The ASSISTANT PRINCIPAL'S HANDBOOK

The ASSISTANT PRINCIPAL'S HANDBOOK
Strategies for Success

JEFFREY GLANZ

CORWIN PRESS
A Sage Publications Company
Thousand Oaks, California

For information:

Corwin Press
A Sage Publications Company
2455 Teller Road
Thousand Oaks, California 91320
www.corwinpress.com

Sage Publications Ltd.
1 Oliver's Yard
55 City Road
London EC1Y 1SP
United Kingdom

Sage Publications India Pvt. Ltd.
B-42 Panchsheel Enclave
Post Box 4109
New Delhi 110 017 India

Printed in the United States of America

Library of Congress Cataloging-in-Publication Data

Glanz, Jeffrey.
The assistant principal's handbook: Strategies for success / Jeffrey Glanz.
    p. cm.
Includes bibliographical references and index.
ISBN 0-7619-3102-3 (cloth) — ISBN 0-7619-3103-1 (paper)
    1. Assistant school principals—United States. 2. School management and organization—United States. I. Title. LB2831.92.G43 2004
371.2´012—dc22   2003026756

This book is printed on acid-free paper.

        05   06   10   9   8   7   6   5   4   3   2

Acquisitions Editor:	Robert D. Clouse
Editorial Assistant:	Jingle Vea
Production Editor:	Diane S. Foster
Copy Editor:	Mary L. Tederstrom
Typesetter:	C&M Digitals (P) Ltd.
Proofreader:	Scott Oney
Indexer:	Teri Greenberg
Cover Designer:	Michael Dubowe
Graphic Designer:	Lisa Miller

Contents

Preface

Top 10 Reasons to Become an Assistant Principal

10. It's not a job, it's an adventure!

9. Get "invited" to all dances, club meetings, home games, etc., etc.

8. Discipline . . . what a concept!

7. You get to be in charge when the principal is away.

6. Interesting collection of confiscated items.

5. Daily visits from the "BEST" students in the building.

4. You can interpret unusual hand signals.

3. Good practice for professional wrestling career.

2. Bus duty, lunchroom duty, hall duty . . . all yours.

1. Finally, join the ranks of the administration.

Linda A. Vollmer (www.lovetoteach.com)

The first nationwide research study of the assistant principalship was conducted by the National Association of Elementary School Principals (NAESP, 1970). The research study surveyed 1,270 assistant principals (APs) and simply developed a composite of the "average" AP. Data were collected on various characteristics of APs as well as information about their experience, training, functions, financial status, and working conditions. The purpose of the study was not a critical analysis of the assistant principalship, but rather a descriptive overview. The major contribution of the study was that it highlighted the importance of the assistant principalship.

In an attempt to uncover more information about the role and function of the AP, I conducted a survey some time ago. Parenthetically, the results of this survey have been confirmed numerous times since. My sense was that APs were

Form P.1   Respond

Article I. RESPOND

What are the roles and responsibilities of assistant principals (APs)?

Take a look at the list of duties below.

1. Rank them in terms of what you think APs actually do in schools (i.e., award a #1 to the duty you think APs do most frequently, #2 for the next most frequent duty, etc.).
2. Rank them, in your view, in terms of their degree of importance (i.e., #1 to the duty APs should be engaged in, #2 to the next most important duty, etc.).

Compare your responses to the results of my study explained in the Preface.

Duties	What APs Actually Do	What APs Should Do
Student discipline Lunch duty School scheduling (coverages*) Ordering textbooks Parental conferences Assemblies Administrative duties Articulation** Evaluation of teachers Student attendance Emergency arrangements Instructional media services Counseling pupils School clubs, etc. Assisting PTA Formulating goals Staff development (inservice) Faculty meetings Teacher training Instructional leadership Public relations Curriculum development Innovations and research School budgeting Teacher selection		

*Coverages refers to scheduling substitute teachers to cover for absent regular classroom teachers.
**Articulation refers to the administrative and logistical duties required to prepare for graduation (e.g., preparing and sending cumulative record cards for graduating fifth graders to the middle school).

not usually charged with leadership responsibilities including curriculum and staff development, teacher supervision, classroom observation, and creation of new instructional programs, research, and evaluation. Rather, they were burdened by routine administrative tasks, custodial duties, and discipline matters.

Although my study (Glanz, 1994b) was limited to almost 200 New York City APs, many of my colleagues around the country confirmed that my results reflected their perceptions and experiences of the roles and responsibilities of APs in schools (also see Weller & Weller, 2002).

The primary research questions that this study attempted to answer were

1. What are your current responsibilities as an AP?

2. In your view, what duties should APs be performing?

3. What aspects of your job give you the greatest satisfaction?

See if the findings below match your responses to the Respond (Form P. 1). Data gleaned from the study revealed the following:

1. Table P.1 lists various duties respondents indicated that they performed. Rankings, not of importance but of major responsibilities, are noted, as well as percentages of APs who performed the duties. More than 90% of the respondents indicated that their chief duties included handling disruptive students, dealing with parental complaints, supervising lunch duty, scheduling coverages, and completing surveys, forms, book orders, and other kinds of administrative paperwork. Curiously, APs in this survey were significantly underinvolved in staff development, teacher training, and curriculum development.

2. Nearly all the respondents reported dissatisfaction with the practices noted in Table P.1. They indicated that their job was "thankless" and that morale was low, although 55% of the APs explained that working with selected teachers and students brought them much satisfaction. Note some of the comments offered:

> The mindless tasks I perform daily really disturb me. In college I trained to do staff and curriculum development. Here on the job I'm responsible for paperwork, lunch duty, and discipline. . . . I derive little satisfaction from these duties.

> Endless paperwork, hall patrol, and especially guarding a gate really inspire me to do my best. [sarcasm]

> I feel underutilized. My expertise seems to be wasted with inane matters. This job is thankless, with little satisfaction.

Working with the children and teachers gives me the greatest satisfaction. Helping a child or teacher succeed is really nice. When I can resolve a troublesome instructional problem I enjoy my job.

3. More than 90% of the APs stated that they preferred working on the following responsibilities: teacher training, curriculum development, and staff development. These APs lamented the fact that they have little time to devote to these important duties given the exigencies of the assistant principalship (see Table P.2). It appears that although APs maintained that certain duties should remain in the purview of the principal (e.g., teacher selection, budgeting, and public relations), a majority of those surveyed indicated that APs should be involved in more "professional and fulfilling" responsibilities.

Table P.1   Actual Duties of Assistant Principals: Rankings and Percentages

Duties	Rank	%
Student discipline	1	94
Lunch duty	2	95
School scheduling (coverages*)	3	91
Ordering textbooks	4	93
Parental conferences	5	91
Assemblies	6	91
Administrative duties	7	91
Articulation**	8	90
Evaluation of teachers	9	83
Student attendance	10	71
Emergency arrangements	11	63
Instructional media services	12	54
Counseling pupils	13	46
School clubs, etc.	14	41
Assisting PTA	15	35
Formulating goals	16	32
Staff development (inservice)	17	27
Faculty meetings	18	24
Teacher training	19	24
Instructional leadership	20	23
Public relations	21	9
Curriculum development	22	7
Innovations and research	23	5
School budgeting	24	3
Teacher selection	25	1

*Coverages refers to scheduling substitute teachers to cover for absent regular classroom teachers.
**Articulation refers to the administrative and logistical duties required to prepare for graduation (e.g., preparing and sending cumulative record cards for graduating fifth graders to the middle school).

Table P.2   Assistant Principals' Rankings of Their Duties for Degree of Importance

Duties	Rank	%
Teacher training	1	93
Staff development (inservice)	2	92
Curriculum development	3	91
Evaluation of teachers	4	90
Instructional leadership	5	90
Formulating goals	6	86
Innovations and research	7	83
Parental conferences	8	82
Articulation	9	82
School scheduling (coverages)	10	81
Emergency arrangements	11	80
Assemblies	12	80
Administrative duties (paperwork)	13	76
Instructional media services	14	68
Counseling pupils	15	61
Faculty meetings	16	55
Ordering textbooks	17	51
School clubs, etc.	18	45
Assisting PTA	19	39
Student attendance	20	34
Student discipline	21	31
Lunch duty	22	25
Public relations	23	21
School budgeting	24	11
Teacher selection	25	9

4. 99% of the respondents stressed the importance of the assistant principalship. At the same time, they complained that they rarely engaged in professional activities such as instructional supervision, program development, and evaluation procedures. As one AP noted: "I went to graduate school to complete certification by focusing on theories and research about instructional supervision, yet most, if not all, of my time is spent on mundane and mindless administrative routines, like lunch duty." Interestingly, approximately 70% of the respondents reported that student discipline and supervision of lunch duty should not be the foci of APs.

Based on this and similar studies, I would like to raise a major point about the role and responsibility of APs that sets the tone for *The Assistant Principal's Handbook*. The nature of public schooling is too complex today to expect one person to single-handedly administer, supervise, and reform schools. There must be instructional leaders, other than the principal. Our first task, then, is to redefine the AP's role with an emphasis on more significant involvement in instructional and curricular improvement. This, of course, entails relieving the AP of, for example, lunch duty and serving as chief disciplinarian. As Ann Hassenpflug (1991), in an article published in *Education Week* titled "A Wasted Reform Resource: The Assistant Principal," stated,

> If the assistant principal doesn't prowl the hallways looking for rule-breakers, who will? Certainly, the responsibility for student attendance and discipline needs to be assigned to school personnel, but just because these tasks have always been assigned to assistant principals doesn't mean that is the way it always has to be. The tasks could be divided among other types of staff members who might actually be more appropriately trained to handle the social and emotional aspects of students' behavior. (p. 23)

The question of who will be responsible for supervising discipline is an important one and should be addressed. Perhaps, as in many middle, junior, and senior high schools, a dean of discipline specially trained to manage the social and emotional aspects of students' behavior can be instituted in elementary schools. Delegating responsibility to specially trained personnel will not relieve the AP of all disciplinary matters. It will, however, extricate the AP so that he or she can be involved in more instructional matters.

Similarly, additional personnel can be assigned to cover lunch duty responsibilities. A teacher-in-charge can deal with the day-to-day operations of lunch duty, and the AP can supervise the program by making spot checks, conferring with assigned personnel, and establishing regulations.

Partially relieving APs from these duties will have a threefold effect: (1) It will allow more time for staff development planning or simply assisting teachers in the classroom; (2) morale will improve by allowing APs to engage in more creative and intellectually stimulating instructional/curricular activities; and (3) academic and social objectives will have a greater chance of being achieved because more time will be allotted for instructional improvement.

Although I believe that APs must be given greater opportunities for instructional leadership and curriculum development, I have devoted sufficient attention in *The Assistant Principal's Handbook* to some of the more mundane duties of APs, such as school discipline and administrative concerns, simply because change is difficult, and many APs are still involved in these noninstructional duties. Still, I have included important instructional and curricular skills that more and more APs are engaging in thanks to insightful principals, school boards, and other concerned policymakers.

You've purchased this book because you are an educator who understands the importance of the assistant principalship. Perhaps you are a teacher considering becoming an AP in the near future, or maybe you've just begun your first year or two in the position. Perhaps you're a longtime AP who wants to learn more about your role as instructional leader. Maybe you're a principal who wants to utilize your AP in the best way possible to promote instructional leadership. Other readers may include professors who prepare future school administrators and supervisors. Other readers might include staff developers, superintendents and their assistants, school board members, board of education officials, and other interested educators.

Many books on becoming a principal flood the market. Rarely does someone become a principal, however, before serving as a vice or assistant principal. Yet few if any books address the unique needs of prospective and practicing assistant principals. Few books exist that actually address the very *practical* issues an assistant principal faces or will face. There are some books that study the assistant principalship from a theoretical viewpoint, and a few of them even attempt to give the reader a glimpse into the "life world" of an assistant principal. But again, few, if any, specifically address the day-to-day responsibilities of the role. *The Assistant Principal's Handbook* is a book that presents and describes the very practical issues of assistant or vice principals. The book culls the essential principles and ideas about the assistant principalship in an easy-to-read, concise manner.

The Assistant Principal's Handbook includes the following features:

- Each chapter begins with *Focus Questions* that encourage thoughtful attention to key elements within the chapter.
- Several chapters include a questionnaire or some self-assessment instrument to stimulate thought on the particular issue or topic.
- Scattered throughout the text are activities to challenge you to reflect or to respond to a particular idea or set of ideas (as in the Respond earlier).
- Also scattered throughout the text are what I call "In-Basket Simulations." It is a study technique I derived from an approach used when I studied for licensure as an assistant principal and principal in New York City. The approach was developed by the Institute for Research and Professional Development (http://www.nycenet.edu/opm/opm/profservices/rfp1b723.html). Scenarios that you as an AP are likely to encounter are presented for your reaction. For instance, "A letter from an irate parent complaining that a teacher hit her child is sent to your attention. What would you do?" Challenging you to confront real-life phenomena under controlled conditions, these simulated in-basket items will prompt critical inquiry.
- Vignettes that provide a realistic glimpse into the life of an assistant principal.

- Resources include the following components:
  - *Annotated Bibliographies* highlight "must reads" for assistant principals
  - *Best Web Sites for Assistant Principals*

The Assistant Principal's Handbook includes the following chapters:

1. Past and Present Challenges to Assistant Principals as Instructional Leaders. A look into the origins of the assistant principalship and a discussion of an intractable problem faced by APs as instructional leaders.

2. Essential Knowledge, Skills, and Dispositions. Drawing from the vast literature on leadership in general, and supervision and curriculum specifically, this chapter identifies some essential knowledge, skills, and dispositions that form the basis for work as an assistant principal.

3. Clinical Supervision. Basic primer on using the clinical supervision cycle, including teacher observation.

4. Instructional Improvement. Basic primer on promoting instructional improvement by working with teachers on teaching strategies that promote student achievement.

5. Curriculum. Basic primer on curriculum development.

6. Program Development and Evaluation. Practical strategies for establishing and conducting an evaluation of any school program.

7. Why Didn't They Teach Me This Stuff in Graduate School? Assistant principals may have taken courses in supervision and curriculum in graduate school, but the realities of the job require assistant principals to serve as chief disciplinarians and lunchroom/bus duty coordinators. This chapter describes the skills necessary to deal with schoolwide discipline and administrative exigencies. This chapter will also provide some concrete suggestions for the following items: developing a master schedule, the AP's role in special education, strategies for running effective meetings, and methods for involving parents.

8. Do I Want to Remain an Assistant Principal? Brief discussion of the assistant principalship as a career or as a path to the principalship.

Acknowledgments

I didn't always want to write this book. In fact, I didn't always want to be an assistant principal. No one grows up hoping to become an assistant principal. One may hope, perhaps, to become a doctor, lawyer, accountant, principal, or teacher, but not an assistant principal. The assistant principalship, however, is an important school position: a rite of passage for aspiring principals or a career for unique individuals. After about ten years of teaching I knew I wanted to one day serve my school as an assistant principal. I would like to acknowledge those individuals who have inspired my own work as an assistant principal and who I recall fondly and respectfully as I write this book.

Harold Gilbert was a master teacher, a compassionate human being, and a competent supervisor. When I was a teacher, his shrewd guidance and advice helped me survive those early years of teaching. I recall his deep sense of professionalism and distinguished appearance. I looked up to him and always wanted to be like him. I did write him a note of thanks for all his support; unfortunately, after four years of teaching I was transferred from that school and never saw him again—although I did call him years later to tell him I was an assistant principal, but I haven't spoken to him since. However, as I write this acknowledgment, I know I owe him much.

I served in a number of other schools and witnessed the efforts of several assistant principals. I experienced the bureaucrat, the elder statesman, the disciplinarian, and the confidant. All served nobly, with zeal, commitment, and skill, each in his or her own way. I would like to mention Norma Adams, who as I write serves as a principal in New York City. At the time we worked together, however, she served with me as an assistant principal in a large elementary school in Brooklyn, New York. A K–5 inner-city school, P.S. X served 1,500 students. I was in charge of Grades 4 and 5 with more than 500 students, while Norma served Grades 2 and 3. She too was an inspiration, although her style of leadership and manner were very different from mine. Yet, she represented the very best of the assistant principalship, and as I write this book I think about her innovative ideas and actions. She was the first to teach me how to deal with school politics. I have not since met a woman or man shrewder or more insightful.

I would like to thank and acknowledge Ronald L. Evans, who selected me as one of his assistant principals. As principal of P.S. X, his support of my ideas helped me develop and grow into the position of AP: I learned from his expertise and insights. I sincerely appreciate the letters he wrote me acknowledging my work and positively reinforcing my performance during my early years as an AP.

Thanks also to Dr. Patricia Celso, a professor at my institution, for her ideas on special education. Thanks to Dr. Thomas Montero, from whom I learned many of the ideas covered in this book in my attempt to earn New York state certification as a principal and assistant principal. His in-basket ideas and ideas in Chapter 7 on dealing with several administrative exigencies such as cafeteria duty were formative. Many thanks to Robb Clouse, senior editor at Corwin Publishers, who believed in this project and my ability to make it happen. I owe a great deal to many other individuals who have contributed to the publication of this book. While I certainly acknowledge their contributions, any deficiencies that exist are my sole responsibility.

Corwin Press gratefully acknowledges the contributions of the following individuals:

John W. Davis
Assistant Principal
Malibu High School
Malibu, CA

Susan Nakaba
Associate Principal of Curriculum & Technology
Palos Verdes Peninsula High School
Rolling Hills Estates, CA

Randy Shuttera
Assistant Principal
Neptune Middle School
Kissimmee, FL

Janice Zuege
Assistant Principal
Hortonville Middle School
Hortonville, WI

About the Author

Jeffrey Glanz received his BA and MS from the City University of New York and an MA and EdD from Teachers College, Columbia University. He formerly taught at the elementary and middle school levels for fifteen years before serving as an assistant principal in an urban elementary school for nearly five years. He taught at the secondary level as well as in other nonformal school settings. Dr. Glanz currently serves as dean of graduate studies (http://www.wagner.edu/graduate/message.html) and chair of education (http://www.wagner.edu/dept/education/) at Wagner College in Staten Island, New York. He holds faculty status as a tenured professor in the Department of Education. Dr. Glanz was executive assistant to the president at Kean University and was named Graduate Teacher of the Year in 1999 by the Student Graduate Association. He was also the recipient of the Presidential Award for Outstanding Scholarship in the same year. Dr. Glanz has authored ten previous books on various educational topics, including coauthoring *Supervision That Improves Teaching* and *Supervision in Practice* (2nd edition) with Corwin and his previous Corwin book, *Teaching 101: Classroom Strategies for the Beginning Teacher*. He is a prominent national speaker on topics that include instructional leadership, educational supervision, and teaching strategies. You may contact him at jglanz@wagner.edu. View his Web site at http://www.wagner.edu/faculty/users/jglanz/web/

**CORWIN
PRESS**

The Corwin Press logo—a raven striding across an open book—represents the union of courage and learning. Corwin Press is committed to improving education for all learners by publishing books and other professional development resources for those serving the field of K–12 education. By providing practical, hands-on materials, Corwin Press continues to carry out the promise of its motto: **"Helping Educators Do Their Work Better."**

1

Past and Present Challenges to Assistant Principals as Instructional Leaders

The full range of the Assistant Principal's (AP's) responsibilities and the demands made on APs remain largely invisible to most who come into contact with them.

—Hartzell, Williams, & Nelson, *New Voices in the Field, The Work Lives of First-Year Assistant Principals*

♦

FOCUS QUESTIONS

1. What comes to mind when you think of an assistant principal?

2. How did the position emerge in schools?

3. What value is there in understanding the origins of the assistant principalship?

4. What impact can an assistant principal have on the life of a teacher? A student?

5. Can you work with teachers as colleagues even though you have a stake in their evaluation? Explain why or why not.

Carl Glickman once referred to supervision as the "glue" that binds a school together. Although not a very appealing metaphor, "glue" does accurately communicate the importance of an assistant principal (AP) to a school. Undervalued and often unacknowledged, the AP is the often unseen, yet cohesive element that contributes to an efficient and effective school. Much literature has focused on the principalship as vital for successful school success (see, e.g., Lipham, Rankin, & Hoeh, 1985; Lucio & McNeil, 1969; Robbins & Alvy, 2003; Schumaker & Sommers, 2001). Less attention has been given to the role and function of the AP (Gorton & Kettman, 1985). Attesting to this neglect, Timothy J. Dyer (1991), executive director of the National Association of Secondary School Principals (NASSP), explained:

> There was a time, in the not-too-distant past, when the assistant principal was not accorded much attention in the literature or on the job. Very little was said about the APs job in university training programs, and almost nothing was said about it in professional books or journals. The AP was simply regarded as someone employed—if the school's enrollment justified it—to take some of the burden off the principal. (p. 58)

The Assistant Principal's Handbook is based on the premise that the assistant principalship is a vital resource for instructional improvement and overall school success. Despite its lack of attention in the literature compared to the principalship, the assistant principalship has been seen as a valuable asset to the school organization (Calabrese & Tucker-Ladd, 1991; Glanz, 1994a, 1994b; Hartzell, Williams, & Nelson, 1995; Marshall, 1992; Pellicer & Stevenson, 1991; Simpson, 2000). Traditionally, the AP was a person in charge of disciplinary and selected administrative matters. Today, greater attention is being focused on the expansion of the AP's role and function to include curriculum and staff development as well as instructional leadership (Calabrese, 1991).

Although the assistant principalship has attracted interest of late (Koru, 1993), we know very little about the origins of the position in schools. Understanding these origins may help us to better understand current problems. Our image of the past is also important in framing future possibilities for these important school leaders.

EARLY DEVELOPMENTS LEADING UP TO THE EMERGENCE OF THE ASSISTANT PRINCIPAL

Throughout most of the nineteenth century, schools were controlled by loosely structured, decentralized ward boards. Superintendents and principals had little authority to effect educational policy and implement meaningful programs or curricula (Gilland, 1935; Reller, 1935). In the late nineteenth century, however, educational reformers sought to transform schools into a tightly organized and efficiently operated centralized system. These reform efforts brought order and organization to an otherwise chaotic, corrupt, and inefficient school environment (Glanz, 1991). It was during this tumultuous period of time that educational decision making was vested in the superintendency. Daily control of the schools was assumed chiefly by superintendents.

In the first two decades of the twentieth century, schooling grew dramatically. Between 1895 and 1920 total school enrollment increased from 14 to 21.5 million students. During the same period, the high school and above population grew from about 350,000 to 2,500,000 students. In 1895 there were slightly more than 398,000 teachers, earning an average annual salary of $286. The number of female teachers was more than double that of their male counterparts. By 1920, in comparison, the total number of teachers increased by more than 280,000 while their salary more than doubled. There were more than five times the number of female than male teachers (U.S. Bureau of the Census, 1960).

The tally of principals and other supervisory personnel only began after 1900. Before this time, supervision was controlled chiefly by the superintendent, with little authority delegated to assistants and principals. After 1900, as urbanization intensified and the school system was growing more complex, the superintendent lost contact with the day-to-day operations of the schools. As a result, supervision of schools after 1900 became the responsibility of the school principal, a person known as the "principal" teacher.

The principal as school leader and chief supervisor gained in stature and authority in the early twentieth century. Although present in the nineteenth century, the principal did not wield any power or significantly affect the nature and character of schooling. The principal in the nineteenth century was essentially relegated to the relatively noninfluential position of "head teacher." Not until after about 1920 was the principal relieved of teaching duties. As Willard S. Elsbree and E. Edmund Reutter (1954) point out, the principal, up until the 1920s, would "take over classes on occasion, and demonstrate to the teacher exactly how the job should be done" (p. 231). The principal's primary duties were concentrated on offering assistance to less experienced teachers in areas such as instruction, curriculum, and general classroom management skills. In the late nineteenth century the principal was expected to obey the directives of city superintendents. In fact, it was the superintendent who usually appointed an individual "principal" or head teacher. There were no fixed criteria for selection as a principal in the late nineteenth or early twentieth century. Selection as principal was based on presumed excellence in teaching and essentially was determined by the whim of the superintendent. The principal was given little authority to do more than complete attendance and other administrative reports.

As schooling expanded so did the educational bureaucracy, with the number of principals doubling between 1920 and 1930. Educators accounted for this increase with industrial metaphors. Elsbree and Reutter (1954) explained the role and function of principals as follows: "The principal was looked upon as a kind of foreman who through close supervision helped to compensate for ignorance and lack of skill of his subordinates" (p. 231). Due to increasing administrative duties, however, the principalship gradually shifted away from direct inspections, classroom supervision, and instructional development, and assumed a more managerial position. Consequently, other supervisory positions were established to meet the demands of a growing and increasingly more complex school system.

Special and General Supervisors

In addition to the building principal, a new cadre of administrative officers emerged, assuming major responsibility for day-to-day classroom supervision. Two specific groups of supervisors were commonly found in schools in the early twentieth century. First, a "special supervisor," most often female and chosen by the building principal with no formal training required, was relieved of some teaching responsibilities to help assist less experienced teachers in subject matter mastery. Larger schools, for example, had a number of special supervisors in each of the major subject areas. In the 1920s and 1930s, some schools even had special supervisors of music and art.

Second, a "general supervisor," usually male, was selected not only to deal with more "general" subjects such as mathematics and science, but also to "assist" the principal in the more administrative, logistical operations of the school. The general supervisor, subsequently called assistant principal, would prepare attendance reports, collect data for evaluation purposes, and coordinate special school programs, among other administrative duties.

Differences in functions between special and general supervisors were reflective of prevalent nineteenth-century notions of male-female role relationships. Note the remarks made by a prominent nineteenth-century superintendent, William E. Chancellor (1904): "That men make better administrators I have already said. As a general proposition, women make the better special supervisors. They are more interested in details. They do not make as good general supervisors or assistant superintendents, however" (p. 210). Representative of the bias against women in the educational workplace were notions espoused by William H. Payne (1875), author of the first published textbook on supervision: "Women cannot do man's work in the schools" (p. 49). Payne, like many of his colleagues, believed that men were better suited for the more prestigious and lucrative job opportunities in education.

It is also interesting to note that special supervisors were more readily accepted by the ranks of teachers than were general supervisors. Special supervisors played a very useful and helpful role by assisting teachers in practical areas of spelling, penmanship, and art, for example. In addition, these special supervisors really did not have any independent authority and did not serve in an evaluative capacity as did, for example, the general supervisor, who was given authority, albeit limited, to evaluate instruction in the classroom. Therefore, teachers were not likely to be threatened by the appearance of the special supervisor in the classroom. The general supervisor, on the other hand, was concerned with more administrative and evaluative matters and was consequently viewed as more menacing to the classroom teacher. Special supervisors also probably gained more acceptance by teachers, most of whom were female, because they too were female. General supervisors were all male and perhaps were perceived differently as a result. Frank Spaulding (1955), in his analysis of this time period, concurred and stated that general supervisors "were quite generally looked upon, not as helpers, but as critics bent on the discovery and revelation of teachers' weaknesses and failures, . . . they were dubbed Snoopervisors."

The position of the special supervisor did not endure, however, for a very long period in schools. The duties and responsibilities of the position were gradually, yet steadily, usurped by general supervisors. Although a detailed explanation of why the special supervisor became obsolete is needed, the relative obscurity of the position after the early 1920s can be attributed to discrimination based on gender. Because most were females, special supervisors were not perceived in the same light as were general supervisors, principals, assistant superintendents, and superintendents, who were, of course, mostly male. Gender bias and the sexual division of labor in schools go far toward explaining the disappearance of the special supervisor as such.

Sex-role stereotypes in education as a whole were commonplace and in consonance with bureaucratic school governance. Not only were curriculum and instruction standardized, but hiring, promotion, and salary scales were also routinized. Along with the newly emerging bureaucratic hierarchy in the early 1900s came the expansion of managerial positions, which were almost always filled by men. This is not very surprising given the previously mentioned views on women held by leading educators of the time. Myra Strober and David Tyack (1980) explained that widely held views of patriarchal dominance were consistent with structured forms of control highly valued by urban school reformers. They explained the relationship between gender and social control as follows:

> By structuring jobs to take advantage of sex role stereotypes about women's responsiveness to rules and male authority, and men's presumed ability to manage women, urban school boards were able to enhance their ability to control curricula, students and personnel. . . .

RECOLLECTION

I recall my dissertation research, as I studied school supervision historically (Glanz, 1991). I came across an anonymous poem published in a magazine called Playground and Recreation *in 1929. The poem was titled "The Snoopervisor, The Whoopervisor, and The Supervisor." As I write today, I think about this poem and ask you, the reader, to consider which role you'd want to play?*

With keenly peering eyes and snooping nose,
From room to room the Snoopervisor goes.
He notes each slip, each fault with lofty frown,
And on his rating card he writes it down;
His duty done, when he has brought to light,
The things the teachers do that are not right.

With cheering words and most infectious grin,
The peppy Whoopervisor breezes in.
"Let every boy and girl keep right with me!
One, two, three, four!
That's fine! Miss Smith I see.
These pupils all write well. This is his plan.
Keep everybody happy if you can."

The supervisor enters quietly,
'What do you need? How can I help today?
John, let me show you. Mary, try this way.'
He aims to help, encourage and suggest,
That teachers, pupils all may do their best.

Rules were highly prescriptive. . . . With few alternative occupations and accustomed to patriarchal authority they mostly did what their male superiors ordered. . . . Difference of gender provided an important form of social control. (p. 35)

In short, general supervisors gained wider acceptance simply because they were men.

With the disappearance of the special supervisor in the early thirties, the general supervisor was the principal's primary assistant. By the forties and fifties, the literature more accurately reflected the relationship between the principal and the general supervisor by using the title "assistant principal."

APs were selected by principals from the ranks of teachers. Less often, they were appointed by the superintendent and assigned to a principal. APs were subordinate to principals and were seen as advisers with little, if any, independent formal authority. The AP was often warned "not to forget that the superintendent runs the whole system and the principal runs his school, and you are merely an expert whose duty it is to assist. . . ." (Sloyer, 1928, p. 429).

Lessons Learned

Given the fact that the assistant principalship originated as an administrative function, it is not very surprising that the primary responsibilities of APs have generally centered on routine administrative tasks, custodial duties, and discipline. APs have not usually been charged with instructional responsibilities, in large measure due to the historical antecedents that led to the development of the position in schools. General supervisors, and later APs, were traditionally charged with noninstructional issues. Curiously, although special supervisors were, in fact, responsible for more instructional concerns, such as the improvement of instruction, their duties were not assumed by the newly titled AP. Efforts under way today to expand the role of the AP to include instructional leadership can certainly be historically linked to the emergence of the early *special* supervisors.

REFLECT

Think of the APs you have known. Were they male or female? How does gender impact on the assistant principalship? What has the history of the assistant principalship described above taught you? Why is knowing this history important to your practice as an AP?

_____

_____

_____

_____

_____

A Problem for APs as Instructional Leaders

Although efforts are under way nationally, at least over the past several years, to involve APs less in administrative, logistical matters and more with instructional matters (Weller & Weller, 2002), a seemingly intractable problem still faces APs; that is, the improvement versus evaluation dilemma. Put succinctly, APs are faced with a basic role conflict. They, by the very nature of their positions in the school hierarchy, are authorized to enforce organizational mandates and ensure administrative efficiency. Among other things, one of the responsibilities frequently assigned to APs is evaluating teachers, or at least making recommendations to the principal about evaluation. On the other hand, many are simultaneously responsible for promoting teacher effectiveness and student learning. Herein lies the conflict: the unresolved dilemma between the necessity to evaluate and the desire to genuinely assist teachers in the instructional process.

Role conflicts of this nature have been documented by Catherine Marshall (1992) in her comprehensive study of APs. Marshall stated that "an assistant principal might be required to help teachers develop coordinated curricula—a 'teacher support' function." "But this function," explained Marshall, "conflicts with the monitoring, supervising, and evaluating functions. . . . The assistant may be working with a teacher as a colleague in one meeting and, perhaps one hour later, the same assistant may be meeting to chastise the same teacher for noncompliance with the district's new homework policy." Marshall concluded, "When they must monitor teachers' compliance, assistants have difficulty maintaining equal collegial and professional relationships with them" (pp. 6–7).

This inherent role conflict, experienced by many APs that I personally know, has been documented by other prominent scholars as well. Tanner and Tanner (1987), in their noteworthy and scholarly textbook on school supervision, acknowledge this dilemma. Although not discussing APs specifically, Tanner and Tanner's analysis rings true to the experiences I have encountered as an AP. Supervisors are challenged daily, they say, to assist teachers "in solving classroom problems" (p. 105). As such, they are inclined to interact with teachers personally and professionally. To be effective leaders, APs maintain friendly, helpful relationships with teachers. However, when evaluations must be done, these collegial relationships may be jeopardized. Tanner and Tanner observed, "No doubt, many teachers are afraid to ask for help from supervisors because they believe that by exposing a problem with their teaching, they are inviting a low evaluation of their work" (p. 105). They stated that this role conflict is inherent in supervisory work. They called it a "basic conflict" between "inservice education" and "evaluation" (pp. 105–6).

As an AP in a large urban school in New York City, my primary function was to serve as a disciplinarian. Our school attempted to restructure governance and redefine role expectations of APs and teachers under a plan known as site-based management. As a result, my role as AP was refocused as primarily concerned with "improving" the instructional process on the grades I supervised. Parenthetically, we created a new position, "dean," whose primary function was to serve as disciplinarian. An important part of my job was to assist and advise teachers on how best to improve instruction and promote learning. After all, "supervision is about helping people grow and develop. . . . It is the job of the supervisor in schools to work with people to improve the educational process and to aid the growth and development of students" (Wiles & Bondi, 1991, p. 85).

Although I was quite satisfied with my instructional responsibilities, I realized that a dilemma was emerging. I was still charged with evaluating the effectiveness of teachers. As an evaluator, I had to make judgments as to their effectiveness. Teachers were observed formally and informally. Observation reports were placed in teachers' files and used for promotional and tenure considerations. APs, as evaluators, are at times perceived by teachers as intrusionary bureaucrats or "snoopervisors" (Hill, 1992, p. v; see also Glanz, 1989) and are met with resentment. Consequently, teachers may be unwilling to ask for assistance because the AP is seen as an adversary. Teachers are reluctant to willingly seek help from an AP for fear that they will be evaluated unsatisfactorily. Costa and Guditus (1984) observed that supervisors are often confronted with the task of having "to evaluate and assist in dismissing incompetent teachers." They contended that this evaluation process tends "to interfere with the helping relationship needed to work productively with other staff members" (p. 24).

Tanner and Tanner (1987) asserted that the conflict between the "helping" and "evaluative" functions present almost insurmountable problems for supervisors. As a former AP, I can personally attest to this problem. Tanner and Tanner stated, "The basic conflict between these functions is probably the most serious and, up until now, unresolved problem in the field of supervision" (p. 106; also see Liftig, 1990).

RECOLLECTION

Improvement Versus Evaluation: One Case Example

P.S. X was located in Brooklyn, New York. It was built in 1905 and was a large elementary school serving approximately 1,500 pupils (kindergarten through Grade 5). The school was administered by a principal and three

(Continued)

(Continued)

assistant principals. It was identified, in 1990, by the New York State Department of Education as a school "in need of assistance" as a result of low scores in reading at the third-grade level. The 1990–91 pupil ethnic survey provided the following data about the school's student population: African American 85%; Hispanic American 10%; Asian American 3%; and Other 2%. The socioeconomic data indicated that 95% of the students were eligible this year for free lunch.

P.S. X was located in a district that had traditionally accepted bureaucracy as the primary authority for supervisory policy and practice. Therefore, as described by Sergiovanni (1992), teachers were subordinates in a hierarchically arranged system, were expected to comply with predetermined standards, and were, among other things, directly supervised and closely monitored to ensure compliance to bureaucratic mandates. Within this system, it was not surprising to find APs, for example, whose role expectations and performance on the job conformed to districtwide bureaucratic rules and regulations.

My first appointment as an AP was at P.S. X. When I arrived, I was greeted by my predecessor. Mr. Stuart Oswald Blenheim (fictitious, of course) was known as a stickler for every jot, tittle, and iota inscribed in the Board of Education's rules and regulations. He actually carried a tape measure, stethoscope, and portable tape recorder as he daily patrolled the hallways. He informed me at our first meeting that teachers were, by and large, incompetent and could not be trusted.

Mr. Blenheim's daily plan was to patrol the corridors to catch wandering pupils who did not have appropriate documentation. He would escort them to class where he would then check if the windows in the room were opened no more than six inches, which was the amount prescribed by Board of Education regulations. He also routinely made certain that teachers were maintaining pace with the Comprehensive Instructional Mathematics Services (CIMS) math program, which was mandated by the district. He checked plans on the desk, observed the aim written neatly on the board, and as he left would utter comments into his small, pocket-sized recorder. Teachers would frequently receive a follow-up letter describing any and all infractions of Board of Education policy.

It was an unwritten law in the school that any teacher who observed this latter-day Napoleon lurking in the halls would, duty-bound, pass the information on to his or her neighbors. A note referring to "Pearl Harbor,"

"Incoming Missiles," or "Sneak Attack" was enough to raise blood pressure and churn digestive juices.

Such was Blenheim's repute that all the teachers whom I supervised avoided my presence like the very plague. On one occasion, I passed by a room and noticed a teacher caringly assisting a pupil at her desk. Suddenly, the teacher "felt" my presence, quickly straightened her posture, and proceeded nervously to the front of the room to resume writing on the board. I soon realized the problem and couldn't blame them.

During the first meeting with my teachers, I asked rather than told them not to think of me as their supervisor. I hoped that they would consider me a colleague with perhaps more experience and responsibility in certain areas. I wanted to share my knowledge with them. I wanted to work with them, help them, assist, guide, coach, collaborate. . . . I was not going to spy on them. They had a difficult time accepting this. They had not only experienced what one teacher called a "petty tyrant" but also indicated that many APs they had had in this and other schools were not unlike Mr. Blenheim. Even "those nice APs" still, in the words of one teacher, "evaluated us and were just picayune."

Several teachers asked if I was required to evaluate them several times a year. I informed them that I was required to, but they would find me fair and even-handed. I told them I would never base my evaluation on merely one observation. We would work together, I told them, and mutually arrive at an acceptable evaluation schedule and policy. We would do our best to cooperate and coexist. I would help them teach more effectively, share my experiences, and readily accept their expertise and ideas. Despite my reassurances, I sensed their doubts and apprehensions.

Teachers later shared their apprehensions about the AP/teacher relationship. Many teachers, for example, stated that they hesitated asking for assistance from APs fearing negative evaluations. In my school, several teachers confided in me a year and a half later that they felt uncomfortable about working closely with APs who might "form negative opinions about me while working on the curriculum committee." "I prefer to stay away from my AP . . . I never know when I'll be written up."

My intention here is not to address the pervasiveness of the improvement versus evaluation conflict, but merely to provide personal testimony to its existence and indicate that through gradual trust building much can beaccomplished. As APs who work with teachers on instructional improvement projects, you must be aware of this problem and find personal ways

(Continued)

(Continued)

to circumvent it. For me, involving teachers on shared decision-making councils, conferring with teachers, asking their input, and treating them as colleagues had a beneficial effect on how teachers perceived me as their AP. As one teacher put it: "I now know that Blenheim is gone."

What shared leadership and collaborative planning do is to develop trust. Involving teachers in collaborative planning (e.g., curriculum and even budget meetings) demonstrates to them our commitment to partnership and shared governance. Teachers realized, as a result of our collaborative efforts at P.S. X, that we all had a stake in working together to attain our shared goals.

Suggestions for APs as Instructional Leaders

An examination of the history of supervision, in general, indicates a gradual move away from "bureaucratic inspectional approaches to more refined democratic participatory" practices (Sullivan & Glanz, 2000, p. 21). Democratic supervision, as embraced by APs for instance, is centered on working with teachers in a collaborative environment to help them improve instruction. Although vestiges of the bureaucratic legacy remain (were they reflected in your personal images from the Reflect exercise), APs as instructional leaders in their own right can overcome the negative images of their past and can develop strategies to resolve the improvement-evaluation dilemma. Following are some suggestions:

- **Acknowledge the past and articulate a vision for the future.** Realize that the position you hold and even your actions are rooted in a past with which you were not involved. Therefore, people may react to you, at least initially, based on their experiences with former supervisors or with assumptions about the role of AP (recall Blenheim in the previous Recollection). Make it clear through words and deeds that your vision for school improvement is rooted in democratic, participatory instructional leadership.

- **Create a democratic learning community.** Imagine new ways of viewing learning. Learning is no longer conceived as predictable but rather as a complex and differentiated process. Teaching moves from simply rote methods to informed reflective judgments. Supervision is no longer concerned with ensuring adherence to bureaucratic regulations but is concerned with helping

teachers discover and construct professional knowledge a
and supervisors are no longer isolated and independent t
collegial team members, mentors, and peer coaches. Sc
bureaucratic teaching organizations, but rather are dem
learning communities.

- **Serve as a role model by encouraging collegiality.** Several individuals within the system will still try to adhere to the old industrial model
based on an obedient workforce that was predisposed to following orders from
above. As you know, schools are too complex for such isolated decision making to persist. You realize the importance of allowing others to assume more
responsibility and to participate fully in shared decision making. Avoiding
impersonal or bureaucratic relationships in favor of encouraging personal
relationships within a learning community can be one of your foremost
contributions.

- **Support shared governance opportunities.** Encourage others to
aspire to democratic leadership by facilitating teacher empowerment and developing democratic structures and processes in a variety of school contexts (e.g.,
peer-coaching activities, school-based leadership teams to revise curricula, etc.).

- **Focus on fundamental instructional issues.** Although you are
cognizant of the many political complexities that affect a school or district,
focus on what really matters to students—instruction. Strive to encourage good
pedagogy and teaching. Faculty and grade meetings should focus almost exclu-
sively on instructional issues.

- **Communicate an "ethic of caring."** Improve your listening skills.
The next time a staff member has experienced a personal challenge, ask her or
him about what happened. Listen, say you're sorry, and offer to help in any way.
That's it; that's all you should or could do. Also, inspire all those you meet to
aspire to excellence. Offer them the means to do so by providing appropriate
resources and suggestions, if they inquire.

- **Empower others and give them the credit.** As a confident leader
you feel comfortable in empowering others to participate in school improvement initiatives. You lead by example and are ready, willing, and able to stand
in the background to allow others to take the credit. As long as you are attain-
ing your objectives, you should not be concerned about receiving all the credit.
You realize that a good leader is one who can empower others to share their
leadership qualities in order to achieve a "greater good."

- **Build trust by your actions.** No matter what you articulate, in writing or in speech, teachers and others will always rely on your actions to speak
for themselves. Can they trust you? Do you talk the talk *and* walk the walk?

IN-BASKET SIMULATION

During an interview you are asked the following questions:

- What would you do to encourage teachers to trust that you are there to "help" them and not merely to "evaluate" them? (Here are some suggested solutions merely offered to get you started: Tell them so; show them so by not writing an evaluation that includes information gleaned during one of your "helping" sessions; help them at every opportunity; get them some extra monies/supplies to support classroom instruction; etc.)

- How would you forge a role for yourself as an instructional leader and not merely a manager, especially in a school in which the former APs did not focus on instruction? (Here are some suggested solutions: Allot time for instructional involvement with faculty; conduct a demonstration lesson for them occasionally; discuss teaching and learning with them on many occasions; conduct workshops on various topics of teacher interest, and bring in speakers to discuss instructional issues; etc.)

Here are suggestions to guide you as you complete this in-basket exercise and all the others to follow in *The Assistant Principal's Handbook*:

1. Think and respond as if you are an AP, not a teacher or, perhaps, principal.

2. Place yourself mentally in each situation as if the case were actually happening to you.

3. Draw on your experiences and from what you've learned from others. Think of an AP you respect and ask yourself, "What would Mr. X have done?"

4. In your response, include the principal (after all, you're her or his "assistant"). That said, there are situations in which you might want to handle the situation yourself without consulting (bothering) the principal. What are some circumstances in which you would have to consult the principal? See the following suggestions.

5. Involve parents and community whenever feasible and applicable.

6. Make distinctions between actions you would personally take and actions you would delegate to others.

7. Utilize resources (personnel or otherwise) to assist you.

8. Think about your response, and then share it with a colleague for her or his reaction.

9. Multiple correct responses are possible, but know that some responses to these scenarios might not be appropriate. See the Recollection in Chapter 2 in which I responded inappropriately to a real-life situation when I was an AP.

10. Record your response and then a day later reread the scenario and your response. Would you still have reacted the same way?

Times when you should consult the principal:

- Any serious incident involving the media
- Any time the daily schedule is interrupted due to a special event, an emergency, a dangerous situation, and so on
- A chronic situation in which you need principal support, such as a major complaint by a parent, an unsatisfactory teacher, a school hazard, and so on
- Faculty/staff concerns
- District/community concerns
- Whenever a board member talks with you

Can you think of other situations in which you should consult the principal?

2

Essential Knowledge, Skills, and Dispositions

Quality education in the schools requires excellence in its leaders.

—Adapted from Michael Fullan

---◆---

FOCUS QUESTIONS

1. What essential knowledge, in your view, should an AP possess?

2. What necessary skills should an AP possess?

3. What dispositions or values are important for serving as an AP?

4. What aspects of your job give you the greatest satisfaction?

5. Has your training prepared you for the realities of the assistant principalship? Explain.

Schools are more complex than ever before and demand more "sophisticated sets of skills and understandings than ever before" (Lambert, 1998, p. 24). For these reasons, among others, it is imperative that educational leaders, including and especially APs, possess competencies deemed necessary for success in their field (Calabrese, Short, & Zepeda, 1996). The literature recognizes that the role of the leader, in general, has three interrelated domains: educational leadership, managerial competency, and political/leadership ability. Each of these domains involves philosophical, social, and psychological perspectives, as well as technical competencies. Unprecedented changes in our community and society at large are adding to the complexity of these dimensions. Although the latter two domains are necessary, the former is most crucial (see, e.g., Ubben, Norris, & Hughes, 2000) for leaders in the twenty-first century. This "educational leadership" domain requires expertise in the following areas:

- Foundations/Philosophy
- Learning
- Teaching/Instruction
- Curriculum
- Research
- Teacher supervision
- Instructional evaluation
- Staff development
- Program evaluation

REFLECT

Which essential knowledge, skills, and dispositions (values) are important for assistant principals? Drawing on recollections of past APs as well as your personal expectations, note in each following category specific knowledge, skills, and dispositions you possess or want to possess. Compare your responses to the information in the next section.

Knowledge

_____

_____

_____

Skills

_____

_____

Dispositions

_____

_____

Drawing from the vast literature in leadership in general, and supervision and curriculum specifically, I have identified essential **knowledge**, **skills**, and **dispositions** that form the basis for the information in the rest of this book. Knowledge involves competence in content areas and the ability to articulate philosophies, attitudes, and beliefs that guide the practice of assistant principals (Fenstermacher, 1994). Skillful APs use a variety of instructional, curricular, managerial, and leadership strategies. APs possess unique dispositions that undergird their work with teachers, students, parents, and the principal. What knowledge, skills, and dispositions should APs possess?

Before I engage you in identifying knowledge, skills, and dispositions, I think it's necessary to consider and consciously express your beliefs about your work and your aspirations: that is, what do you hope to accomplish? Doing so will lay the foundation for living up to the knowledge, skills, and dispositions discussed in this chapter. The following two exercises (one Reflect and one Respond) are meant to stimulate your thinking.

REFLECT

Imagine that it's your retirement dinner. For this celebration the following colleagues have been invited to relate what you have meant to them and to relate your contributions to the school during your tenure as an AP: a teacher, a fellow AP, and a principal. What would you want them to say about you? Jot down your ideas in the space below. Read on, and we'll analyze your responses.

_____

_____

(Continued)

> (Continued)
>
> _____
>
> _____
>
> _____
>
> _____

Form 2.1   Respond

<table>
<tr><td colspan="5" align="center">Article I. RESPOND</td></tr>
<tr>
<td>SA = Strongly Agree ("For the most part, yes")
A = Agree ("Yes, but . . .")
D = Disagree ("No, but . . .")
SD = Strongly Disagree ("For the most part, no")</td>
<td>SA</td>
<td>A</td>
<td>D</td>
<td>SD</td>
</tr>
<tr><td>1. I feel upset when others criticize or belittle teachers and teaching.</td><td></td><td></td><td></td><td></td></tr>
<tr><td>2. The reason why I became an assistant principal and remain one is because I love to supervise others.</td><td></td><td></td><td></td><td></td></tr>
<tr><td>3. I consider those who go into the assistant principalship, for the most part, committed and dedicated professionals.</td><td></td><td></td><td></td><td></td></tr>
<tr><td>4. I would like to become a principal one day.</td><td></td><td></td><td></td><td></td></tr>
<tr><td>5. I went into the assistant principalship, for the most part, because of the increased sense of prestige.</td><td></td><td></td><td></td><td></td></tr>
<tr><td>6. I became an assistant principal to get out of the classroom.</td><td></td><td></td><td></td><td></td></tr>
<tr><td>7. I became an assistant principal as a way to earn more money.</td><td></td><td></td><td></td><td></td></tr>
<tr><td>8. I think that most teachers are competent.</td><td></td><td></td><td></td><td></td></tr>
<tr><td>9. Assistant principals really run the school.</td><td></td><td></td><td></td><td></td></tr>
<tr><td>10. In order to be a good assistant principal, one should also have been a good teacher.</td><td></td><td></td><td></td><td></td></tr>
</table>

Let's discuss some of your responses to these activities:

- So, it's your retirement dinner. What would you want your colleagues to say about you? I bet not one of you wrote, "He taught me how to write a lesson plan" or "She really organized that assembly program fantastically." When we think about it, what really matters is how we treat others as individuals, as human beings. You more likely want your colleagues at your retirement dinner to recall how you treated them with respect, never raised your voice in anger, encouraged them, promoted justice and opportunity for all, helped teachers do a better job, or exhibited school spirit and dedication to students beyond the call of duty. These are the true reasons that we go into education and the assistant principalship. Certainly, managing school programs, organizing a multicultural fair, developing a school safety plan, and overseeing school cafeteria duty are important and essential. But, what matters most are those dispositions or values we impart intentionally or unintentionally. These endearing values and virtues reflect our character and our impact on others. They are what leadership is all about. Don't you agree?

- What about your responses to Respond?

  1. *I feel upset when others criticize or belittle teachers and teaching.* Good supervisors care about teachers and teaching. They realize that their work sets the tone and establishes a conducive environment to support teaching and student learning. APs as school leaders foster a sense of a learning community. They are staunch supporters of the teaching profession.

  2. *The reason why I became an assistant principal and remain one is because I love to supervise others.* Wanting to help others is admirable. If you interpreted this statement in its ideal sense then "loving to supervise others" is a lofty pursuit. However, those who go into administration and supervision primarily for the prestige or for the accompanying authority of the position do not do a service to themselves or those whom they work with.

  3. *I consider those who go into the assistant principalship, for the most part, committed and dedicated professionals.* Working long hours, putting up with the politics of the job, dealing most of the time with complaints from students, teachers, and parents are usually not very pleasant responsibilities. Yet, dedicated APs are professionals who perform an invaluable service in schools.

  4. *I would like to become a principal one day.* As I will discuss in the final chapter, those who aspire to the principalship will find work as an AP

satisfying and a wonderful learning experience. Still, the assistant principalship should be viewed as an honored career in its own right.

5. *I went into the assistant principalship, for the most part, because of the increased sense of prestige.* It's perfectly normal to admit that you might have aspired to a supervisory position because of the increased prestige associated with school administration. Unfortunately, we work in hierarchical organizations that award greater prestige to those who supervise and administer than to those who teach. Administrators and supervisors earn more money and are awarded more privileges than teachers. Until society's values change and teachers gain greater stature than they currently hold in the educational system, positions in administration will have greater prestige. Although administrative positions offer much prestige, one hopes that you became an AP to fulfill a personal and professional need, the need for service to the profession.

6. *I became an assistant principal to get out of the classroom.* Assistant principals in my estimation should be teachers of teachers who can offer their experience and expertise to improve teaching and learning. If you became an AP simply to "get out of the classroom," one hopes that either you'll mature and grow into the position to realize the importance and value of the classroom teacher or you'll leave the profession.

7. *I became an assistant principal as a way to earn more money.* Who doesn't want to earn more money? Although administration does offer greater financial incentives than does teaching currently, one hopes, as stated in response to the previous question, that your aspirations go beyond the financial.

8. *I think that most teachers are competent.* Good APs appreciate the importance of good teaching and view teachers, for the most part, as competent. I am reminded of some supervisors of old who maintained that teachers were essentially incompetent. In 1891, T. M. Balliet of Massachusetts insisted that there were only two types of teachers: the efficient and the inefficient. The only way to reform the schools, thought Balliet, was to "secure a competent superintendent; second, to let him 'reform' all the teachers who are incompetent; thirdly, to bury the dead" (Balliet, 1891, pp. 337–338). Characteristic of the remedies applied to "improve teaching" was this suggestion: "Weak teachers should place themselves in such a position in the room that

every pupil's face may be seen without turning the head" (Fitzpatrick, 1893, p. 76). Thankfully, we've come very far.

9. *Assistant principals really run the school.* Many APs actually "run" the day-to-day operations of the school. However, a school cannot function well without a competent principal. APs must always realize that their role is as the title implies: that is, they serve to "assist" the principal.

10. *In order to be a good assistant principal, one should also have been a good teacher.* I believe that this statement is true especially if one looks at the work of an AP as an instructional leader.

Your reactions to my responses?

_____

_____

_____

_____

What specific knowledge, skills, and dispositions do you feel are important for serving as an AP? Please note that the list to follow is neither exhaustive nor definitive. Various preparation programs may emphasize different aspects. The following list is drawn from the literature on the assistant principalship along with my understanding of the unique needs of APs in schools.

Knowledge

Models of supervision. The AP possesses knowledge of teaching to engage teachers in instructional dialogue to improve teaching and student learning. Models include clinical, developmental, collegial and collaborative, and mentoring.

Curriculum development. The AP understands the processes and activities that lead to curriculum development and revision.

Leadership. The AP understands varied leadership styles in self and others and understands the importance of involving all stakeholders in solving problems.

Organizations. The AP understands the dynamics of organizational theory and the importance of culture building within the school among students, teachers, and parents.

Assessment, evaluation, and technology. The AP understands and has knowledge of traditional and nontraditional assessment tools, including observation/ evaluation strategies and technological applications.

Skills

Instructional design. The AP can assist teachers in planning instruction based on knowledge of the subject matter, student needs, community, and curriculum goals (including state/district performance standards).

Staff development. The AP can develop and implement an ongoing series of professional development workshops to increase levels of teaching competencies among teachers.

Planning and coordination. The AP understands how to plan and coordinate various school programs.

Instructional improvement. The AP can conduct systematic and comprehensive assessments via classroom observations to provide constructive feedback to teachers for instructional improvement.

Communication. The AP effectively uses verbal and nonverbal communication techniques to foster active inquiry, collaboration, and supportive relationship building skills.

Assessment. The AP uses formal and informal assessment strategies to evaluate and ensure the continuous intellectual development of the teacher. Action research strategies are used to study and improve practice.

Dispositions

Humility. The AP is aware of her or his limitations while at the same time cognizant of her or his abilities. The AP acts as a support and assistant to the principal.

Judgment. The AP demonstrates ability to reach logical conclusions and make high-quality decisions in a decisive manner.

Professional partnerships. The AP commits to collaboration in schools and other learning communities.

Ethical behavior. The AP recognizes ethical implications of educational practices and commits to ethical principles of behavior.

Professionalism. The AP models professional and leadership behaviors in all interactions with school and community.

Do you agree or disagree with the previous list? Explain. What knowledge, skills, or dispositions were omitted in the previous list?

A TYPICAL DAY IN THE LIFE: KNOWLEDGE, SKILLS, AND DISPOSITIONS IN ACTION

Today was a typical day for Ms. Roberta Rodriguez, vice principal of Boynton High School, located in an affluent suburb of Chicago. In addition to preparing the day's scheduling and arranging for substitute teachers, she was involved in many activities associated with her position as vice principal in a large school of nearly 2,500. Today, Ms. Rodriguez's responsibilities involved the following:

- Distributed newly obtained textbooks to the English Department
- Selected Mr. William Johnson to escort the school band to the district's open house celebration
- Decided to call an emergency grade conference to familiarize teachers with the newly adopted core content curriculum standards
- Recommended to the School-Community Council that Ms. Sarah Barnett be selected as Parent of the Month
- Completed her evaluation report of the afterschool student-at-risk program
- Began a needs assessment in order to implement an interdisciplinary team teaching program
- Placed a new admission in Mr. Steve Goldman's already overcrowded homeroom
- Suggested that the art-science program be revised
- Scheduled time for the Chess Club to meet during Period 4
- Recommended suspension for Maurice and Christopher for pulling the fire alarm at dismissal
- Interviewed a prospective teacher for a vacancy in the English Department
- Oversaw first period lunch duty in the cafeteria
- Recommended to the principal that Ms. Joan Smith, an untenured teacher, not be rehired for the next semester
- Observed Ms. Phyllis Williams, a veteran teacher, during the fourth period
- Conducted a postconference with Ms. Williams during the eighth period
- Helped grade teachers plan a curriculum unit

- Reached out to community leaders to raise money to paint the walls of the fourth floor
- Spoke, in the evening, to the school board about various instructional and curricular projects her teachers had established

As you can see, Ms. Rodriguez's day, like those of most other educational leaders, was not only arduous and frenetic at times, but also filled with many varied situations. Without possessing specific knowledge, skills, and dispositions unique to the assistant principalship, Ms. Rodriguez could not effectively carry out her responsibilities.

Develop a plan to build your competence in the previously stated knowledge, skills, and dispositions. What do you need to do in order to accomplish your plan?

Chapters 3 through 6 will deal with specific knowledge and skills that are essential for good APs: clinical supervision, instructional improvement, curriculum, and program evaluation.

One of the essential dispositions for leaders is ethical behavior. Read the recollection that follows. How would you have acted?

RECOLLECTION

The following is not a personal recollection but one shared with me by a close friend and colleague, who as an AP was confronted with a dilemma that tested an important disposition: ethical behavior, and maybe even his courage.

"Mr. Melnick, I want to speak to you about an urgent matter. I know you are in the process of. . . ." Interrupting himself, Dr. Speer, president of the school board, asked if Gerry could meet him for lunch at noon. Hesitating a moment to review his daily calendar, he responded affirmatively. To Gerry's surprise, rather than eating in the district office cafeteria, Dr. Speer invited him out to one of the finest local restaurants in town. Reluctantly, he consented. During their almost one-and-one-half hour lunch, Dr. Speer, dominating much of the conversation, reviewed Gerry's past achievements and articulated his vision for the future. "We have much that remains to be accomplished," explained Dr. Speer. "We will construct this new addition to the high school, we will build a new sports facility. . . ." Although Gerry appreciated his lofty

construction projects on behalf of the district he silently wondered why he was asked for lunch. After all, he was not all embroiled in district politics over these construction efforts. "What does he want from me?" he wondered. Then the reason for the meeting became apparent.

"Mr. Melnick, my nephew has applied for the teaching position. Although he is a new graduate, he is intelligent and enthusiastic. He has the right stuff to become a great teacher. I'd appreciate it if you would consider him for the position. I realize that the principal has the ultimate say, but she will follow your strong recommendation." Gerry recognized the name as one of the applicants and assured Dr. Speer that he would be given all fair consideration along with all the other candidates. Of course, this was not what Dr. Speer wanted to hear.

Sitting more erectly in his chair, he leaned closer to Gerry and said, "Let me be clearer, a bit more explicit. I'd really appreciate your help in this matter." He then abruptly asked for the check and escorted Gerry back to the office. The conversation in the car ride back to the office centered on recent national news items. Thanking him for this "important lunching opportunity to get to know you better," Dr. Speer dropped him off by the entrance and then breezed down the street in his Lexus. Aghast at Dr. Speer's crassness and temerity, he didn't inform even his closest friends and colleagues, nor the principal, about what had happened.

Ruminating about this circumstance over the next several days, he received several other calls from the board president on unrelated matters. "Umm," he thought to himself, "he never called me before about anything." The interviews were completed over the following week and Dr. Speer's candidate was clearly inferior to the others. He knew that this new position was critical. The person filling the position had to replace his best and most experienced teacher who was retiring. He knew which candidate deserved the job offer. He spent several days longer than he would have ordinarily done to consider the candidates. Finally, he made up his mind.

Mindful of the consequences, he did not select Dr. Speer's nephew. The new candidate assumed his position, and weeks passed without his ever hearing again from Dr. Speer. Later, Gerry applied, as he does every year, for released time to attend a national conference. This time he received a written note from the principal that his request was denied.

On several other occasions, Gerry was similarly refused released time for various events. On one instance, he had to use his sick leave to

(Continued)

> (Continued)
>
> *attend a local workshop. Weeks later, when district funds were curtailed for his professional development projects, his indignation turned to anger and resentment. He fully realized what was going on.*
> *What would you have done in a similar situation?*

These next two response activities help you assess your dispositional levels in two areas mentioned earlier.

Form 2.2   Respond

Article II. RESPOND			
SA = Strongly Agree ("For the most part, yes") *A = Agree ("Yes, but . . .")* *D = Disagree ("No, but . . .")* *SD = Strongly Disagree ("For the most part, no")* ***SA A D SD***			
1. I do not flaunt my accomplishments. I do not like to be acknowledged for what I have done. I do not necessarily consider myself more competent than other educational leaders.			
2. I do not deserve recognition and/or deference from others due to my training, knowledge, and experience.			
3. I alter my beliefs when evidence is presented to contradict them.			
4. I experience feelings of doubt about my job performance.			
5. I usually welcome and accept criticism easily.			
6. I usually admit ignorance and would say "I don't know" when I really didn't know something.			
7. I have several limitations but try to accentuate my strengths.			
8. Without my leadership assistance, things could get accomplished.			

Explanation

1. I do not flaunt my accomplishments. I do not like to be acknowledged for what I have done. I do not necessarily consider myself more competent than other educational leaders.

Humble leaders will attest to these three ideas. Obviously, the same ideas might apply to someone who lacks confidence and possesses low self-esteem. What, in your estimation, is the difference between an individual with high and low self-esteem in regard to the virtue of humility?

2. I do not deserve recognition and/or deference from others due to my training, knowledge, and experience.

Humble leaders do not stand behind their qualifications and demand respect. Rather, they engender respect because they don't look for it. They exude confidence and modesty and others appreciate these qualities in turn.

3. I alter my beliefs when evidence is presented to contradict them.

Stubbornness and refusal to accept alternate viewpoints despite the evidence to the contrary are signs of arrogant individuals. Humble leaders are able to admit mistakes and alter their views because they are self-confident and realize their fallibility and limitations.

4. I experience feelings of doubt about my job performance.

Experiencing doubt at times is normal and is a sign of a humble leader. Never resting on their laurels, humble leaders strive for ways of improving their practice. Feeling doubt will impel them to consider options and suggestions from others. Obviously, if one continually feels doubt then he or she lacks self-confidence and may exhibit low self-esteem.

5. I usually welcome and accept criticism easily.

Humble leaders are confident, reflective practitioners who sincerely want to implement the best pedagogy and practices. Therefore, they are willing to accept advice from many quarters. A humble leader believes that he or she can learn from anyone, even a first-year teacher.

6. I usually admit ignorance and would say "I don't know" when I really don't know something.

Again, I think I've made the point. Do leaders you know readily admit mistakes?

7. I have several limitations but try to accentuate my strengths.

Humble leaders are self-aware. They acknowledge their strengths and limitations.

8. Without my leadership assistance, things could get accomplished.

Humble leaders realize that everyone is expendable.

Are you humble? (see first disposition)

Form 2.3   Respond

Article III. RESPOND				
SA = Strongly Agree ("For the most part, yes") *A = Agree ("Yes, but . . .")* *D = Disagree ("No, but . . .")* *SD = Strongly Disagree ("For the most part, no")*	*SA*	*A*	*D*	*SD*
1. I do not have a problem rendering a decisive decision once I have weighed all the facts of a situation.				
2. One of my major strengths, and confirmed by people I know, is that I am a good judge of character.				
3. I value openness to participation, diversity, conflict, and reflection.				
4. I am committed to consensus building.				
5. I work very hard to develop evaluative criteria to measure attainment of stated objectives.				
6. I have no problem delegating authority in the form of areas of responsibility to capable subordinates and then holding them accountable for results.				
7. I don't jump to conclusions and really try to judge everyone favorably				
8. I am mentally and emotionally centered in order to think clearly about the best course of action to take, even in the face of criticism, insults, nagging, or negativity.				

Explanation

1. I do not have a problem rendering a decisive decision once I have weighed all the facts of a situation.

Do you weigh all the available evidence before rendering a decision? When you have weighed all the evidence can you then move forward decisively?

2. One of my major strengths, and confirmed by people I know, is that I am a good judge of character.

The ability to "read" people is an invaluable asset for a leader, especially in rendering a decision. Can you provide an example of a situation in which you had to do so?

3. I value openness to participation, diversity, conflict, and reflection.

These are critical elements of a leader who makes sound judgments. Can you provide an example in which each of these elements (openness to participation, diversity, conflict, and reflection) has aided your efforts in making a decision?

4. I am committed to consensus building.

Similar to the values expressed in the previous statement, consensus building enables the leader to hear the views of other stakeholders.

5. I work very hard to develop evaluative criteria to measure attainment of stated objectives.

Again, someone who possesses good judgment will work diligently to establish rigorous assessment strategies to assist in decision making.

6. I have no problem delegating authority in the form of areas of responsibility to capable subordinates and then holding them accountable for results.

Identifying appropriate individuals to assume responsibility of major projects and initiatives requires good judgment by a leader.

7. I don't jump to conclusions and really try to judge everyone favorably.

Good judgment requires intelligent reasoning, common sense, and fair play.

8. I am mentally and emotionally centered in order to think clearly about the best course of action to take, even in the face of criticism, insults, nagging, or negativity.

Such emotional and mental stability are essential prerequisites in leadership and are commonly lacking in people with poor judgment.

Do you have good judgment? (see second disposition)

RECOLLECTION

A Case of Poor Judgment

As I was sitting in my office, Mrs. Watts charged in and demanded to see me. As an assistant principal my day is hectic and arduous. The parent complained that Mrs. Klein had struck her child. Despite the fact that I had a report due to the principal at 3:00 P.M. and also had to complete an attendance report for the district office by the next day, I realized that this parent needed my attention. I stopped my writing and gave her my full attention. [Ah, good judgment on my part. Too bad it was short-lived.]

About ten minutes into our conversation (I had barely calmed down the parent), I received a call from Ms. Bryant, the special education teacher, that Shameile was "hanging out of a window on the fourth floor." "So, what's new?" I said to myself. I told Ms. Bryant that I would be up as soon as I could. Not knowing what the call was about, Mrs. Watts continued her tirade against this teacher who allegedly struck her child. She even said, "Wait till I get my hands on her." Our conversation continued for ten more minutes. I finally succeeded in allaying her apprehensions and she agreed to let me investigate the matter and get back to her tomorrow. Relieved that Mrs. Watts was leaving the building and that she had decided not to confront Mrs. Klein, I then turned my attention to Shameile.

By the time I reached the fourth floor, the principal was already there chastising the student for his antics. I dispersed the crowd that had formed around Shameile. The principal, holding Shameile by the collar, told me to follow him to his office. In private, the principal chastised me for not immediately "dropping what I was doing" (talking with Mrs. Watts) to deal with a potentially life-threatening situation on the fourth floor. Even though Shameile had repeated this behavior several times in the past "just to get attention," he explained that I needed to learn good judgment. "You must discern the difference between what is important [Mrs. Watts and her complaint] and what is urgent [Shameile hanging out of the window]."

As I am writing this true incident I realize how ridiculous it may sound to the reader. But I tell you that at the time, in the midst of the incident, it wasn't so clear or so easy.

Follow-up Questions

1. Have you ever experienced a bout of "poor judgment"? Explain.

2. What did my principal mean by differentiating between what is important and what is urgent? Provide an example or two from your experience.

3. What would you have done in the case I described in the previous Recollection? Are you sure?

3

Clinical Supervision

Supervision in education has long drawn on democratic principles. . . .
Teachers and supervisors must recommit themselves to democratic
values. . . . Clinical supervision can provide the means of translating
democratic values into action, while strengthening teachers' technical
skills, conceptual understanding, and moral commitment.

—Edward Pajak, *Approaches to Clinical Supervision:*
Alternatives for Improving Instruction

◆

FOCUS QUESTIONS

1. What is supervision?

2. How is clinical supervision different from traditional forms of supervision?

3. What would you need to know about clinical supervision in order to be convinced of its efficacy?

4. How might clinical supervision contribute to student learning?

5. How might you as an AP incorporate clinical supervision in your school?

6. How have you been observed as a teacher and how do you observe teachers now that you are an AP?

Bureaucratic and inspectional supervision has evolved since its early days toward more democratic and participatory methods (Glanz, 1998). Today, supervision, as professional practice, is a process that engages teachers in instructional dialogue for the purpose of improving teaching and promoting student achievement. Although some principals do not require APs to be versed in instructional leadership, APs in my view should see themselves (and be seen) as teachers of teachers. This notion is predicated on the condition that APs are excellent teachers themselves and possess the knowledge and skills to communicate good teaching practice to teachers. APs understand how to work with teachers in order to improve teaching and promote student learning. APs can incorporate a variety of instructional improvement strategies including clinical supervision that incorporates purposeful classroom observation of teachers in action, not for evaluative purposes but to engage teachers in instructional dialogue about classroom practice. APs are instructional leaders in their own right.

Clinical supervision, as a model of supervision developed thirty years ago, grew out of the dissatisfaction with traditional educational practice and supervisory methods (see Sullivan & Glanz, 1999, Chapter 1). Robert Goldhammer (1969), one of the early progenitors of clinical supervision, stated that the model for clinical supervision was "motivated, primarily, by contemporary views of weaknesses that commonly exist in educational practice" (p. 1). Invented by Morris Cogan (Pajak, 2000), clinical supervision is premised on the notion that teaching could be improved by a prescribed, formal process of collaboration between teacher and supervisor. Clinical supervision focuses on the improvement of instruction by means of systematic cycles of planning, observation, and intensive intellectual analysis during a feedback conference (see Figure 3.1).

Clinical supervision is a superb means for improving teaching and promoting student learning. Assistant principals who want to serve as instructional leaders should become familiar with clinical supervision. To be effective, clinical supervision should be divorced from evaluation. In other words, teachers must be comfortable to share their teaching practices with assistant principals who are trustworthy and will keep any information gleaned confidential. Clinical supervision, if it is to work, must promote instructional dialogue between supervisor and teacher in an open, congenial, and trusting manner. The fundamental premise of clinical supervision is to open up channels of communication, provide feedback to teachers about their teaching in an objective, nonjudgmental manner, and dialogue about teaching and learning.

Here are some suggestions for creating a safe and comfortable environment for clinical supervision implementation:

Figure 3.1   Clinical Supervision Cycle

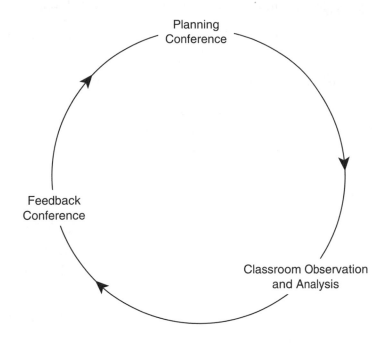

- Never use the clinical supervision cycle for evaluative purposes. In other words, don't place an evaluation letter in a teacher's mailbox that emerged from an observation conducted after clinical supervision.
- Role-play the cycle at a faculty or grade conference in order to demonstrate its use.
- Have an experienced teacher conduct the cycle with you teaching a demonstration lesson. Have it videotaped for viewing at a faculty or grade conference.
- Find occasion to communicate your confidence in the faculty and your commitment to instructional excellence and support of the faculty in every way.

Before we learn and practice the clinical supervision cycle (adapted by Sullivan & Glanz, 1999), it is important to understand that clinical supervision is not only a structure but a concept, and as such, it contains a series of assumptions. Goldhammer, Anderson, and Krajewski (1993) outlined nine major characteristics of clinical supervision that I believe are consistent with any of the approaches and structures in this book:

1. It is a technology for improving instruction.

2. It is a deliberate intervention into the instructional process.

3. It is goal oriented, combining the school's needs with the personal growth needs of those who work within the school.

4. It assumes a professional working relationship between teacher(s) and supervisor(s).

5. It requires a high degree of mutual trust, as reflected in understanding, support, and commitment to growth.

6. It is systematic, although it requires a flexible and continuously changing methodology.

7. It creates a productive (i.e., healthy) tension for bridging the gap between the real and the ideal.

8. It assumes that the supervisor knows a great deal about the analysis of instruction and learning and also about productive human interaction.

9. It requires both preservice training (for supervisors), especially in observation techniques, and continuous inservice reflection on effective approaches. (pp. 52–53)

The Clinical Supervision Cycle

Richard Weller's (1971) formal definition of clinical supervision provides a basis upon which we can develop a cycle of supervision: "Clinical supervision may be defined as supervision focused upon the improvement of instruction by means of systematic cycles of planning, observation, and intensive intellectual analysis of actual teaching performances in the interest of rational modification" (p. 11). Weller referred to the three phases of the clinical supervision cycle as represented in Figure 3.1.

Before I begin to explain each of the three steps in clinical supervision, you should realize that the approach taken for clinical supervision depends on the developmental (Glickman, Gordon, & Ross-Gordon, 1998) level of the teacher. Three distinct approaches to working with individuals include:

- Directive informational
- Collaborative
- Nondirective (self-directed)

These approaches range from somewhat of an AP control to primarily teacher control. The approach the AP chooses is supposed to match the specific teacher's level of development. In reality, many of us tend to favor one approach in our interactions with others. Some supervision systems include a directive control approach in which the AP makes the decision and tells the individual or group how to proceed. Although I agree that "different folks need different strokes" and that varying school circumstances call for a range of approaches, my belief that meaningful learning is dependent on the learner's involvement in constructing that knowledge eliminates the need for the directive control approach. Many APs over the years have used this approach, many continue to follow it, and you may favor it yourself. Nonetheless, I think that the collaborative and nondirective models are the most effective, with the occasional application of a modified directive informational approach.

The AP who uses the directive informational approach frames the choices for the group or individual and then asks for input. In the collaborative approach, the AP and the individual or group share information and possible solutions as equals to arrive at a mutual plan. In the third approach, the AP facilitates the individual or group in developing a self-plan or in making its own decision. Glickman and colleagues (1998), for example, believe that the teacher's level of development, expertise, and commitment and the nature of the situation determine the choice of approach.

The Directive Informational Approach

Key Steps—Directive Informational Approch

1. Identify the problem or goal and solicit clarifying information.

2. Offer solutions. Ask for the teacher's input into the alternatives offered and request additional ideas.

3. Summarize chosen alternatives, ask for confirmation, and request that the teacher restate final choices.

4. Set a follow-up plan and meeting.

This approach is used primarily for new teachers or those who are experiencing difficulties that they do not have the knowledge, expertise, or confidence to resolve on their own or collaboratively. These teachers are seeking or need direction and guidance from an AP who can provide expert information and experienced guidance. Nonetheless, the AP wants the teacher to seek solutions and generate ideas so as to feel at least some ownership of the final choices. Therefore, the AP is the initiator of suggestions and alternatives that the teacher can then revise and refine and to which he or she can add his or her own ideas.

1. Identify the problem or goal and solicit clarifying information.

Avoid small talk and focus immediately on the problem or goal in question. Ask the teacher for clarification of the situation so that you are both sure that you are addressing the same problem or goal.

2. Offer solutions. Ask for the teacher's input into the alternatives offered and request additional ideas.

Even though the new teacher might feel overwhelmed, the AP's ideas will probably stimulate his or her thinking. Offering input and requesting additional ideas will give the teacher a feeling of ownership and allow him or her to begin constructing a personal perspective. Separating the alternatives from the request for additional ideas allows the teacher to think through the suggestions and then come up with modifications or new possibilities.

3. Summarize chosen alternatives, ask for confirmation, and request that the teacher restate final choices.

Verification that both supervisor and teacher have the same understanding of the final choices is crucial. Two people can easily interpret the same words differently or hear different words. Therefore, if each party repeats his or her understanding, any misunderstandings or differences in perceptions can be cleared before action is taken.

4. Set a follow-up plan and meeting.

A concrete plan (written is preferable) and a scheduled meeting are the only ways that two very busy professionals can be sure of the follow-through that is crucial to the success of any plan.

The Collaborative Approach

Key Steps—Collaborative Approach

1. *Identify the problem from the teacher's perspective, soliciting as much clarifying information as possible.*

2. *Reflect back what you've heard for accuracy.*

3. *Begin collaborative brainstorming, asking the teacher for his or her ideas first.*

4. *Problem solve through a sharing and discussion of options.*

5. *Agree on a plan and follow-up meeting.*

In the collaborative approach, the goal is to resolve a problem or reach a goal through shared decision making. The AP encourages the teacher to develop his or her ideas first to allow maximum ownership. Nonetheless, the brainstorming and problem solving are shared, and disagreement is encouraged, with assurances that a mutual solution will be reached. The conference always ends with a restatement of agreed-upon plans and setting of a follow-up meeting. Unresolved issues can be included in the planning process and revisited at the follow-up session.

1. Identify the problem from the teacher's perspective, soliciting as much clarifying information as possible.

With the exception of some new teachers and those with problematic practices, the AP wants the teacher to initiate the discussion from his or her perspective. The more information provided, the clearer the situation for both parties. Therefore, a more complete description can be drawn out with prompts, that is, eye contact and encouraging open body language and nonverbal cues, paraphrasing, probing questions, and phrases such as "Tell me more; Uh-huh; I see; I understand."

2. Reflect back what you've heard for accuracy.

It is crucial that you verify that you've heard accurately the content and perspective of the teacher. A summary of what you understood, with the teacher's verification of what you heard, can avoid many misunderstandings and problems down the road. You may feel like you sound silly repeating everything; rest assured that the teacher is hanging on your every word to be sure that you heard and understood.

3. Begin collaborative brainstorming, asking the teacher for his or her ideas first.

If the AP proposes options first, the teacher might not try to develop his or her own ideas and might just follow what the supervisor suggests. Because the teacher is the one most familiar with the situation, it is important to allow him or her to build on that knowledge or to decide to construct a different or new resolution.

4. Problem solve through a sharing and discussion of options.

One of the greatest challenges to a supervisor in a collaborative approach is to encourage disagreement convincingly. Few teachers are accustomed to administrators fostering challenges and encouraging risk taking. Asking for the teacher's suggestions is a first step. Promoting an open dialogue about the options is the second step.

5. Agree on a plan and follow-up meeting.

In the complex lives of teachers and administrators, a written plan on agreed-upon solutions and those yet to be resolved will save a lot of time in the long run. What often seems time-consuming can be "cost-effective" in the final analysis. Taking the time to write out a plan and set up the next appointment are the essential concluding steps.

The Nondirective Approach

Key Steps—Nondirected Approach

1. Listen carefully to the teacher's initial statement.

2. Reflect back your understanding of the problem.

3. Constantly clarify and reflect until the real problem is identified.

4. Have the teacher problem solve and explore the consequences of various actions.

5. The teacher commits to a decision and firms up a plan.

6. The supervisor restates the teacher's plan and sets a follow-up meeting.

The goal of the self-directed approach is to enable the teacher to reflect on the problem, draw conclusions, and construct his or her own alternatives. The AP serves more as a coach who does not express his or her point of view or ideas unless the teacher specifically requests them. The AP functions as the facilitator of the teacher's development of his or her own ideas. The outcome should always be the teacher's autonomous decision. This approach is appropriate for a very knowledgeable and often experienced teacher. It also can be successful in providing a sense of ownership when the teacher is the primary person responsible for carrying out a decision or when the decision or problem at hand has limited ramifications. A less experienced but creative, promising teacher can also benefit from the guided ownership that this approach affords.

1. Listen carefully to the teacher's initial statement.

As in the collaborative approach, the starting point is the teacher's perspective of the situation. The techniques and prompts are the same as in the collaborative approach: eye contact, body language, paraphrasing, verbal cues, and probing questions.

2. Reflect back your understanding of the problem.

Again, as in the collaborative approach, verification that you have clearly and accurately understood the teacher's perspective is essential. Reflecting back what you have heard begins to accomplish this task. In addition, paraphrasing can clarify any uncertainty the AP may have about what has been expressed and can even allow the teacher to distance himself or herself from what was said and reflect on it from the outside.

3. Constantly clarify and reflect until the real problem is identified.

The crucial prerequisite to solving a problem is to conceptualize accurately what the problem is. Solutions often are hidden in the identification of the problem, thereby limiting the range of resolutions. Thus, the real need must be ascertained. For example, your husband says he's taking the car, and you have a meeting. Your need is not necessarily to take the car, but to find a way to get to the meeting. The facilitator's role is to use the reflecting/prompting/questioning process judiciously to permit the teacher to arrive at a crystallization of the need.

4. Have the teacher problem solve and explore the consequences of various actions.

Once the need has been identified, simply ask the teacher to think of possible alternatives. Assist the teacher in walking through the steps, process, and consequences of each action. Ask questions such as "What would happen if . . . ?" or "How would you . . . ?" Then ask the teacher to explore the advantages and disadvantages of the alternatives. At this point, the teacher may be ready to respond to concluding questions, such as, "Which do you think will work best? Why? In what ways would it be better?"

5. The teacher commits to a decision and firms up a plan.

Once the teacher makes a choice, you can request a plan and encourage a walk-through of the next steps. "What, who, when, how, where" or the provision of simple planning forms that the teacher can complete may be part of the plan.

6. The supervisor restates the teacher's plan and sets a follow-up meeting.

It is important for the supervisor to restate the teacher's plan before ending the meeting. This verification will avoid future misunderstandings. In addition, even though the teacher owns the plan, the scheduling of a follow-up meeting to see how it's working should always conclude the session.

Table 3.1 compares and contrasts the three approaches:

Table 3.1   Approach Comparison

Direct Informational	Collaborative	Nondirective
1. Supervisor identifies problem, then solicits clarifying information	1. Supervisor seeks to identify problem from teacher's perspective	1. Supervisor asks teacher to identify problem
2. Supervisor offers solutions and then requests input	2. Collaborative brainstorming for solutions	2. Clarification and reflection until teacher identifies problem
3. Supervisor summarizes and then asks for confirmation	3. Problem solve through sharing and discussion	3. Teacher problem solves and explores consequences
4. Teacher restates final choices	4. Joint agreement on plan	4. Teacher commits to decision

SOURCE: Sullivan & Glanz, *Supervision That Improves Teaching: Strategies and Techniques*, p. 66. Copyright © 1999 by Corwin Press. Reprinted by permission of Corwin Press, Inc.

With an understanding of three approaches to working with individuals, we are now ready to work through the steps of clinical supervision.

Clinical Supervision Step 1: The Planning Conference

Alisa Hindin, the newly appointed AP of Marlboro Middle School, began her first set of classroom observations as early as possible in the fall. She hoped to develop trusting relationships that would permit her and the teachers to focus on the improvement of teaching and learning, and not on the bureaucratic process of evaluation. She decided to meet with and observe the newest teachers first.

Alisa set up a planning conference with a brand-new language arts teacher. She had heard that Sarah, a recent graduate of a high quality master's program, was having difficulty implementing her student-centered practices. Some of the students had not been exposed to cooperative learning groups before, and rumor had it that some of her classes were out of control. Nonetheless, Alisa decided to query Sarah about what she felt her concerns were. To make Sarah comfortable, Alisa set up a meeting in Sarah's classroom, not in the AP's office.

"Hi, Sarah. How's it going?"

"O.K., I guess."

"Since I will be beginning nontenured teacher observations, I thought we could discuss a particular area, interest, or concern that could be the focus of the observation."

"Gosh, I wouldn't know where to start. You pick it."

"I know that you use a lot of exciting innovative teaching methods. Is there any one in particular that you'd like some feedback on?"

"Mmm . . . I've been trying to have the students work in cooperative groups to discuss their writing, and it doesn't seem to be working in some classes. I have a rambunctious seventh-grade class that doesn't work well in groups at all, and I can't seem to get control of the process. Could you sit in on that class?"

"Sure. Let me show you a couple of tools I could use to observe the groups and see which one you think might pinpoint your concerns."

They decide to use the Cooperative Learning Performance Indicator instrument (see following section) created by Johnson and Johnson.

"What is a convenient time for me to visit when you will be using cooperative groups with the seventh graders?"

"How about third period next Tuesday? They're usually awake by then but not yet completely out of control."

"Fine. Next Tuesday, October 1, third period. While we're at it, could we set a time to meet after the observation? How about during your professional period the following day?"

"Sounds O.K. to me."

"Agreed. Third period on Tuesday and second period on Wednesday. By the way, if you have any other input that would be helpful before I visit, don't hesitate to stop in and share it with me. I'm looking forward to seeing students using this wonderful method."

REFLECT

What does Alisa do to make Sarah feel relaxed and at the same time focus on instruction? How does she get Sarah to reflect on her own perceptions of her needs?

Key Steps—Planning Conference

1. Decide collaboratively the focus of the observation.

2. Determine the method and form of observation.

3. Set the time of the observation and the postconference.

The goals of the planning conference follow:

- To identify teacher interests and concerns in a collaborative manner
- To clarify that the primary purpose of the observation is to improve teaching and learning
- To reduce stress and make the teacher feel comfortable about the process
- To choose an observation tool and schedule the visit and postconference

The three types of planning conferences follow:

1. Decide collaboratively the focus of the observation.

Although the chief purpose of the observation is to improve instruction, it is essential to have the teacher's perspective on his or her concerns and interests. Even a new teacher can help identify the primary or most urgent concerns. Change occurs most easily if the teacher has a role in providing the focus.

2. Determine the method and form of observation.

Once the focus is determined, the supervisor can discuss the appropriate tools. The supervisor will decide whether to include the teacher in making the choice of the observation tool. A newer or less secure teacher may have enough to cope with without taking part in that decision.

3. Set the time of the observation and postconference.

It is important, whenever possible, to provide the teacher with the opportunity to choose the day and time. The teacher knows in which class the focus that he or she has chosen can be observed best. Once he or she has had a role in deciding the focus, the choice is simplified. It becomes a learning experience with less likelihood of the visit being an occasion to put on a show.

Clinical Supervision Step 2: The Observation

The AP understands that teaching is a challenging art and science. Teaching occurs in an incredibly fast-paced environment where hundreds of overt and subtle interactions occur between teachers and students as well as between students and students. Given the complex nature of classroom life (Jackson, 1990), tools for systematically recording classroom interactions are especially useful to assist teachers in understanding more fully and becoming aware of classroom behavior (Good & Brophy, 1997). APs believe that "life in classrooms" is context bound, situationally determined, and complex. The AP is not and should not be the overseer or prescriber but, rather, the guide, facilitator, or collaborator. Relying on enhanced communication and shared understandings, the AP can effectively use observation instruments to encourage interpersonal and collegial relationships. This section does not review all aspects of the varied observation instruments that are possible. For a fuller treatment of varied observation instruments, consult Sullivan and Glanz (1999) and/or Willerman, McNeely, and Cooper-Koffman (1991). However, several tools are described in the following discussion. First, let's review ten general guidelines for any classroom observation.

REFLECT

Describe different kinds of observation techniques or strategies you have personally experienced. Which seemed most effective? Which seemed least effective? What are the primary benefits of the use of observation instruments?

TEN GUIDELINES OF OBSERVATION

Here are several guiding principles about observation that should be kept in mind:

1. Good supervision is about engaging teachers in reflective thinking and discussion based on insightful and useful observation, not on evaluation.

2. Supervision, relying on the use of observation instruments to provide teachers information about their classrooms, is likely to enhance teacher thought and commitment to instructional improvement.

3. Observation is a two-step process: first, to describe what has occurred, and second, to interpret what it means.

4. Too often, we jump into what has been termed the "interpretation trap." We jump to conclusions about a particular behavior before describing that behavior. When we interpret first, we not only lose description of that event, but also create communication difficulties that might result in teacher resistance.

5. The precise observation tool or technique should be chosen collaboratively between teacher and supervisor. However, in most cases, the teacher ultimately should determine the instrument to be used.

6. Observing a classroom is not necessarily an objective process. Personal bias should be acknowledged and discussed. Although two or more individuals may agree on what has occurred (during the description stage), they might interpret its meaning differently. Personal experience, beliefs, and prejudices can lead to misinterpretations. Awareness of the possibility of personal bias is the first step toward interpreting classroom behavior effectively and as objectively as possible.

7. Observing takes skill and practice. Quite often, we interpret as we observe. If these tools of observation are to be effective, then you must practice separating interpretation from description.

8. Be aware of the limitations of observation. No observer can see or notice all interactions. Attempts to do so lead only to frustration and confusion. Start observations in a limited setting with a small group and observe one specific behavior, such as the quality of teacher questions.

9. Disclosure is an essential element for successful observation. Prior to entering the classroom, the observer should discuss with the teacher the following items: where to sit in the room, how to introduce the observer to students, and so on.

10. Don't draw conclusions based on one observation. Teachers have "bad" days, and lessons sometimes don't work. Students too may have "bad" days. Multiple observations with different focuses are necessary.

FOURTEEN TOOLS AND TECHNIQUES FOR OBSERVATION

Table 3.2   Summary of Observation Tools

Quantitative Approaches
  I. Categorical Frequency Tools
        A. Teacher verbal behaviors (Technique 1)
        B. Teacher questions (Technique 2)
        C. Student on-task and off-task behaviors (Technique 3)
 II. Performance Indicator Tools
        A. Gardner's multiple intelligences (Technique 4)
        B. Hunter's steps in lesson planning (Technique 5)
        C. Johnson and Johnson's cooperative learning criteria (Technique 6)
III. Visual Diagramming Tools
        A. Diagram of verbal interactions (Technique 7)
        B. Diagram of teacher space utilization (Technique 8)
 IV. Tailored Tools
        A. Feedback (Technique 9)
        B. Teacher-pupil interaction (Technique 10)
Qualitative Approaches
  I. Detached open-ended narrative tool (Technique 11)
 II. Participant open-ended observation (Technique 12)
III. Child-centered learning observation (Technique 13)
 IV. Nonverbal (Technique 14)

SOURCE: Sullivan & Glanz, *Supervision That Improves Teaching: Strategies and Techniques*, p. 84. Copyright © 1999 by Corwin Press. Reprinted by permission of Corwin Press, Inc.

I. Categorical Frequency Tools

A *categorical frequency tool* is a form that defines certain events or behaviors that can be checked off at frequency intervals and counted. Categories are mutually decided upon by the teacher and the AP.

A. Teacher Verbal Behaviors (Technique 1)

Materials. A watch with a second hand; a Teacher Verbal Behaviors chart (see Table 3.3). Specific behavior is not recorded, merely the fact that the teacher behavior occurred within the time frame.

B. Teacher Questions (Technique 2)

Materials. A watch; a Teacher Questions chart (Table 3.4)

Table 3.3   Teacher Verbal Behaviors

Time Began: _____

	Information Giving	Questioning	Answering	Praising	Direction Giving	Reprimanding/ Correcting
1	x	x	x			x
2	x	x			x	x
3		x			x	
4	x			x	x	
5	x				x	
6		x				x
7	x					
8	x	x			x	
9						
10	x					
11	x				x	x
12						
13						
14	x					
15	x		x			x
16	x				x	x

Time Ended:
Class:

SOURCE: From Carl D. Glickman, Stephen P. Gordon, and Jovita M. Ross-Gordon, *Supervision of Instruction*, 4th ed. © 1998. Published by Allyn & Bacon, Boston, MA. Copyright © 1998 by Pearson Education. Adapted by permission of the publisher.

Special prerequisite knowledge. Familiarity with Bloom's taxonomy

Explanation. AP and teacher collaboratively decide to focus only on the number and quality of questions posed during a prespecified time period. In the case presented in Table 3.4, both teacher and AP agree that Bloom's taxonomy will be used as the principal guide. Six of Bloom's levels are listed: knowledge, comprehension, application, analysis, synthesis, and evaluation. A tally is kept for each instance a question is posed. The observer listens to the question and decides into which of Bloom's categories the tally mark should be made. (Note that your knowledge of Bloom's taxonomy is essential.) At the completion of the observation, totals are computed and percentages are calculated, as noted in Table 3.4. Note that the frequency of each type of question is recorded, but the question itself is not. If the teacher prefers a running record of each question posed, a tape recorder could be used.

Table 3.4   Teacher Questions

Site Practice

Time began: _____

Question Category	Tally	Total	Percent
Evaluation	//	2	7%
Synthesis		0	0%
Analysis	//	2	7%
Application	/	1	4%
Comprehension	////////	8	30%
Knowledge	//////////////	14	52%

Total of questions asked =

Time ended: _____

Class: _____

Date: _____

SOURCE: From Carl D. Glickman, Stephen P. Gordon, and Jovita M. Ross-Gordon, *Supervision of Instruction*, 4th ed. © 1998. Published by Allyn & Bacon, Boston, MA. Copyright © 1998 by Pearson Education. Adapted by permission of the publisher.

Postnote. Note that this type of category frequency tool doesn't necessarily have to deal with "teacher questions." Any behavior that can be tallied may be observed using this format. Can you think of another example of a teacher behavior that can be tallied using this format?

C. Student On-Task and Off-Task Behaviors (Technique 3)

Materials. A watch with a second hand; a Student On-Task and Off-Task Behavior chart (Table 3.5)

Special prerequisite skills. Although using Technique 2 is relatively easy without much practice, we suggest that you practice identifying student on-task and off-task behaviors (Technique 3) prior to actually using the technique in a classroom with a class. Practice is needed because the key used is somewhat complicated. I suggest you memorize and practice using the key prior to any real observation.

Explanation. AP and teacher collaboratively decide to focus on student on-task and off-task behaviors. A list of student names is made as noted in Table 3.5. The students' names are listed according to their seat order beginning from the front row or table and going down each row or table. The observer should

Table 3.5   Student On-task and Off-task Behavior

Time When Sweep Began

Student	9:00	9:05	9:10	9:15	9:20	9:25	9:30	9:35
Tania	A	A	AT	A	A	A	OR	A
Manuel	A	A	AT	AT	A	OR	A	A
Vivian	AT	TK	TK	AT	AT	TK	AT	TK
Nurit	O	O	P	P	OT	O	O	OT
Joseph	OT	OT	AT	P	A	A	P	P
Michael	OT	OT	AT	P	O	AT	A	TK
Loi	AT	P	P	AT	P	P	P	OT
Helen	A	A	A	A	A	A	A	A
Mari/Celi	AT	A	A	A	OR	A	A	A
Wayne	P	P	AT	AT	P	P	OR	OR
Virginia	P	A	A	A	P	AT	A	A
Colleen	OR	A	A	A	TK	O	AT	A
Hajime	OT	OT	OT	OT	OT	OT	OT	OT
Kahlid	TK	AT	A	TK	TK	TK	AT	AT
Maria	OR	A	A	A	TK	A	A	A

Key:
Total:

A = at task
AT = at task with teacher
TK = talking
P = playing
O = out of seat
OR = out of room
OT = off task

SOURCE: From Carl D. Glickman, Stephen P. Gordon, and Jovita M. Ross-Gordon, *Supervision of Instruction*, 4th ed. © 1998. Published by Allyn & Bacon, Boston, MA. Copyright © 1998 by Pearson Education. Adapted by permission of the publisher.

be situated to the side of the front of the room. Because the observer will be seen readily by the students, we suggest that the observer come into the class a couple of times prior to the observation to sit up front and make believe that he or she is taking notes to acquaint students with the observer's presence.

Observations are made in 5-minute intervals (depending on the number of students observed). In our case, fifteen students are being observed. Thus, each student will be watched for 20 seconds (5 minutes = 300 seconds divided by the number of total students being observed [15] = 20 seconds per student). The observer records what he or she sees using the key at the bottom of the chart. Again, familiarity with student on-task and off-task behaviors is essential for this technique to work properly. By the way, the precise on- and off-task behaviors also should be collaboratively developed between observer and teacher.

Postnote. Note that this type of category frequency tool refers to student behavior, whereas the previous two formats referred only to teacher behavior. Can you think of another example of student behaviors for which this technique can be used?

II. Performance Indicator Tools

A *performance indicator tool* allows the observer to record whether or not an action or activity listed on the observation instrument has been observed. Many types of performance indicators are possible. In other words, this tool can be applied to any action or activity that can be observed and recorded. I will provide three examples in which a performance indicator tool may be applied.

A. Gardner's Multiple Intelligences (Technique 4)

Materials. A performance indicator chart keyed to Gardner's eight intelligences (see Table 3.6)

Explanation. Well versed in Gardner's intelligences theory, both observer and observee have collaboratively decided to record the extent to which Gardner's intelligences are incorporated in a fifth-grade science lesson. A prespecified period of time to observe the lesson is agreed upon. The observer merely checks off whether or not the teacher addressed in any way each of Gardner's

Table 3.6   Gardner's Model for Performance Indicators

Elements	Response			Observations
Logical/mathematical	Yes	No	N/A	Mathematical equation examples on board
Bodily/kinesthetic	Yes	No	N/A	No references made
Visual	Yes	No	N/A	Overhead transparencies used
Musical	Yes	No	N/A	No references made
Interpersonal	Yes	No	N/A	No references made
Intrapersonal	Yes	No	N/A	No references made
Linguistic	Yes	No	N/A	Problem-solving examples
Naturalistic	Yes	No	N/A	No references made

Date: 9-28-99
Class: 3-310
Time: 1:15 p.m.

intelligences. The observer may comment on the nature or extent to which each intelligence was introduced and applied.

Postnote. Gardner's theory is only one example for which a performance indicator tool may be applied. Can you think of another example for which this tool may be applicable?

Also, please note that I do not imply that teachers should be "checked" to see whether or not they have incorporated Gardner's theory, or any other theory for that matter. I am merely suggesting that if a teacher *wants* to incorporate Gardner's intelligences, then this performance indicator would be an ideal way to determine whether or not the teacher addressed each intelligence.

B. Hunter's Steps in Lesson Planning (Technique 5)

Materials. A performance indicator chart keyed to Hunter's lesson plan steps (see Table 3.7)

Explanation. Well versed in Hunter's lesson plan model, both observer and observee have decided collaboratively to record the extent to which Hunter's steps are incorporated into a twelfth-grade foreign language lesson. A prespecified period of time to observe the lesson is agreed upon. The observer merely checks off whether or not the teacher in any way addressed each of Hunter's steps. The observer may comment on the nature or extent to which each of Hunter's steps were introduced and applied.

Table 3.7   Hunter's Steps in Lesson Planning

Elements	Response			Comments
Anticipatory set	Yes	No	N/A	No references made
Objective and purpose	Yes	No	N/A	Unstated-unclear
Input	Yes	No	N/A	Group discussion employed
Modeling	Yes	No	N/A	No references made
Checking for understanding	Yes	No	N/A	Teacher asked "Do you understand?" but did not check
Guided practice	Yes	No	N/A	Teacher circulates
Independent practice	Yes	No	N/A	Sample sheets distributed

Date: 9-28-99
Class: 10-406
Time: 11:15 a.m.

SOURCE: From Carl D. Glickman, Stephen P. Gordon, and Jovita M. Ross-Gordon, *Supervision of Instruction,* 4th ed. © 1998. Published by Allyn & Bacon, Boston, MA. Copyright © 1998 by Pearson Education. Adapted by permission of the publisher.

Table 3.8   Johnson and Johnson's Cooperative Learning

Elements	Response			Comments
Explanation of academic and social objectives	Yes	No	N/A	No explanation of either occurred—just went into lesson
Teaching of social skills	Yes	No	N/A	Teacher merely said, "Cooperate"—no instruction
Face-to-face interaction	Yes	No	N/A	Students sitting quietly facing each other
Position interdependence	Yes	No	N/A	One set of responses required from each group
Individual accountability	Yes	No	N/A	None evident—teacher walked around classroom minimally
Group processing	Yes	No	N/A	Students rated their performance

Date: 1/15/04
Class: 4-417
Time: 9:15 a.m.

SOURCE: From Carl D. Glickman, Stephen P. Gordon, and Jovita M. Ross-Gordon, *Supervision of Instruction*, 4th ed. © 1998. Published by Allyn & Bacon, Boston, MA. Copyright © 1998 by Pearson Education. Adapted by permission of the publisher.

Postnote. Again, we are providing only some examples for which a performance indicator tool may be applied. Can you think of another example for which this tool may be applicable?

C. Johnson and Johnson's Cooperative Learning Criteria (Technique 6)

Materials. A performance indicator chart keyed to the criteria applied to cooperative learning (see Table 3.8)

Explanation. Well versed in Johnson and Johnson's cooperative learning format, both observer and observee have decided collaboratively to record the extent to which the criteria of cooperative learning are incorporated in a twelfth-grade foreign language lesson. A prespecified period of time to observe the lesson is agreed upon. The observer merely checks off whether or not the teacher in any way addressed each of the cooperative learning criteria. The observer may comment on the nature or extent to which each cooperative learning criterion was introduced and applied.

Postnote. We are providing only some examples for which a performance indicator tool may be applied. Can you think of another example for which this tool may be applicable?

III. Visual Diagramming Tools

A *visual diagramming tool* portrays what happens visually in the classroom. Several types of visual diagramming tools are possible. Although we present just two examples, please note that others are possible. Also, the uses of video-taping and audio recording, although easily applied to almost any tool, are particularly useful here to provide visual and/or auditory evidence.

A. Diagram of Verbal Interactions (Technique 7)

Materials. A verbal interaction chart outlining the seating arrangement of the particular class being observed (see, e.g., Figure 3.2)

Explanation. A prespecified period of time to observe the lesson is agreed upon. For purposes of analysis in this case, both AP and teacher have agreed upon a 30-minute observation period. Six copies of Figure 3.2 should be made for the observer to record verbal interactions in 5-minute increments: that is, one chart for each 5-minute period. Cross-hatching facilitates the recording of multiple interactions.

Each arrow indicates a complete statement directed to another individual, and the arrows are numbered in sequence. The observer should have extensive experience applying this technique so that recording can proceed smoothly and accurately. Figure 3.2 is provided as a training tool to interpret the verbal inter-action provided.

Postnote. How might the use of audio recording assist or hinder interpretation of the nature of verbal interactions in a lesson?

B. Diagram of Teacher Space Utilization (Technique 8)

Materials. A teacher space utilization chart outlining the room arrangement of the particular class being observed (see, e.g., Figure 3.3)

Explanation. A prespecified period of time to observe the lesson is agreed upon. The observer charts teacher movement around the room and, at the same time, records the times.

Postnote. How might the use of videotaping assist or hinder interpretation of the nature of teacher space utilization?

Figure 3.2   Diagram of Verbal Interaction

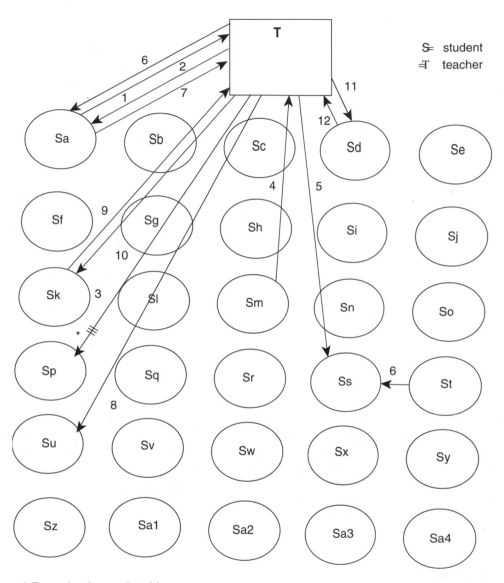

* Example of cross-hatching
Class : 10-517
Date : 11-15-99
Time : 10:15 a.m.

SOURCE: From Carl D. Glickman, Stephen P. Gordon, and Jovita M. Ross-Gordon, *Supervision of Instruction,* 4th ed. © 1998. Published by Allyn & Bacon, Boston, MA. Copyright © 1998 by Pearson Education. Adapted by permission of the publisher.

Figure 3.3   Program of Space Utilization

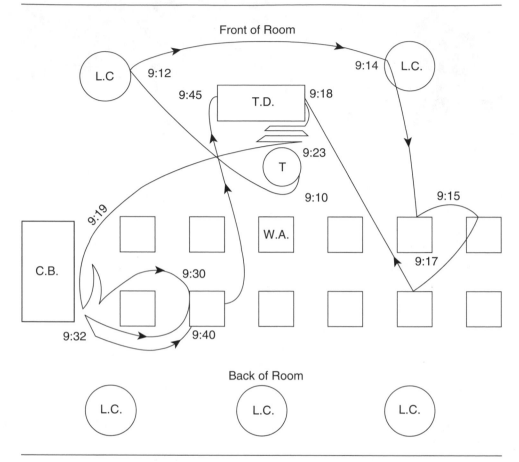

Key: T.D. = teacher's desk; L.C. = learning center; C.B. = chalkboard; W.A. = work area. Note that, of course, the diagram should be drawn for the room in which the observation takes place.

SOURCE: From Carl D. Glickman, Stephen P. Gordon, and Jovita M. Ross-Gordon, *Supervision of Instruction,* 4th ed. © 1998. Published by Allyn & Bacon, Boston, MA. Copyright © 1998 by Pearson Education. Adapted by permission of the publisher.

IV. Tailored Tools

The term *tailored tools* refer to tools especially developed or created based on a teacher's unique concerns. The teacher, in other words, wants the observer to focus on a specific area or areas. Tailored tools fall into the quantitative approach because numerical data are collected.

Many types of tailored tools are possible. As the name implies, these techniques are "tailored" to the needs and interests of teachers. Although I present just two examples, please note that others are possible.

Figure 3.4   Feedback

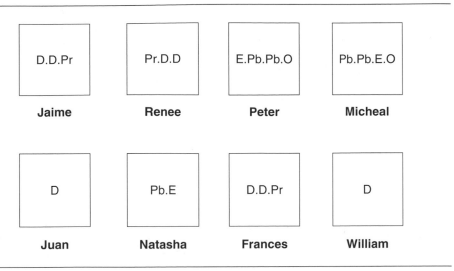

Key: Pr = prompted; Pb = probed; E = encouraged; O = positively reinforced; D = discouraged pupil.

SOURCE: Sullivan & Glanz, *Supervision That Improves Teaching: Strategies and Techniques,* p. 97. Copyright ©
1999 by Corwin Press. Reprinted by permission of Corwin Press, Inc.

A. Feedback (Technique 9)

Materials. A feedback chart outlining the seating arrangement of the particular class being observed (see, e.g., Figure 3.4)

Explanation. A prespecified period of time to observe the lesson is agreed upon.
At a preconference, the teacher informs the observer that he or she is interested
in whether or not he or she prompts, probes, and encourages student responses.
He or she is also interested in how often positive reinforcement is used and how
often pupils' responses are discouraged. A key is then developed collaboratively
by the observer and the observee during the preconference. Once categories
and the key are approved, the observation may be scheduled.

Postnote. Can you develop another chart that might be keyed to another concern that a teacher might have?

B. Teacher-Pupil Interaction (Technique 10)

Materials. A Teacher-Pupil Interaction chart (see, e.g., Table 3.9)

Explanation. In this case, the teacher wants the observer to focus on an
individual student. The teacher informs the observer that he or she is having

Table 3.9   Teacher-Pupil Interaction

Time	Student: *Steve*	Teacher: *Clara Weingarten*
9:05	Disturbing another student	Moves toward Steve
	Ceases misbehavior ◄──	
9:13	Leaves desk; begins ───► wandering around room ──	Establishes eye contact with Steve
	Returns to seat ◄──	
9:18	Playing with friend ───►	Criticizes Steve
	Throws ruler ◄──	Tells Steve to see her after class
	Grumbles under breath ◄──	
9:30	Off task/passive ───►	Approaches Steve, touches him on the shoulder; quietly asks him to go back to his seat
	Back on task ◄──	

Class: 2-517
Date: 11-6-00
Time: 9:00 a.m.

SOURCE: From Carl D. Glickman, Stephen P. Gordon, and Jovita M. Ross-Gordon, *Supervision of Instruction*, 4th ed. © 1998. Published by Allyn & Bacon, Boston, MA. Copyright © 1998 by Pearson Education. Adapted by permission of the publisher.

difficulty with Steve. The teacher complains that Steve's behavior gets progressively worse during a lesson and that the teacher is at his (or her) wits' end. A prespecified period of time to observe the lesson is agreed upon. The observer observes and records the student's behavior as well as noting the teacher's reaction.

Postnote. What other kinds of tailor-made tools can you create?

QUALITATIVE OBSERVATION TOOLS

I. Detached Open-Ended Narrative Tool (Technique 11)

Also known as selective verbatim (Acheson & Gall, 1997) or script taping (Hunter, 1983), the observer records every person, event, or thing that attracts her or his attention. Whatever the observer considers significant is recorded. The observer simply records exactly what is said during the lesson. Not all verbal communications are recorded—only those the observer feels are significant or those communications agreed upon by both supervisor and teacher beforehand. Hence, only selected portions are recorded. Of course, no prearranged categories or questions are developed.

Selective Verbatim

Materials. A notepad or laptop to record observations

Explanation. Supervisor and teacher collaboratively agree that anecdotal evidence will be collected during a prespecified period of time.

OPEN-ENDED NARRATIVE

Fifth-grade class; thirteen boys and twelve girls; self-contained classroom; Amy Clayman, teacher; 9:45 A.M. I enter as Ms. Clayman tells the class to take out their math books. As Ms. Clayman gives instructions for the math assignment, four students (two male and two female) are out of their seats, hanging their clothing in the rear classroom closet. The girl is talking. Ms. Clayman tells her to be quiet and sit down. Teacher takes attendance by reading class roster, name by name. After about 3 minutes, a monitor enters classroom as teacher is recording daily attendance; noise level in class rises. Monitor leaves room. Teacher walks back and forth as students get quiet. At 9:53 A.M., Ms. Clayman asks a girl to tell the class what the answer to the first math problem is. Student responds; class attentive. Ms. Clayman asks a boy, "Can you answer question #2?" Student responds. Teacher calls on a boy who also responds, with a different answer. Ms. Clayman probes and asks boy to explain. Ms. Clayman asks another student to answer the question. Girl responds. Teacher asks another question to a boy and probes. Teacher proceeds this way for the next 15 minutes. Ms. Clayman then asks the class, "How may we figure out how much carpet to buy if the room is 10′ by 15′?" No one raises a hand to answer. Ms. Clayman repeats the question. Still, no response. Teacher draws a diagram on the board and then James calls out, "Oh, I know." Students giggle. Ms. Clayman tells class, "Now, stop that. Pay attention. Go ahead James, tell us." James mumbles something. Ms. Clayman requests that he speak more clearly. James is silent. Teacher then explains to the class how to compute the area of a rectangle. She writes several examples on the board and then calls several students to answer them.

---

1. Describe the unique features of this technique.

2. What must the observer be cautious about when recording observations? Explain.

3. How would you describe what happened during this lesson? Be descriptive in your summary.

4. What conclusions would you draw from this observation?

5. How might you engage the teacher in dialogue about this lesson?

Postnote. The ability of the observer to accurately and quickly record information is essential. Recording such information may appear simple, but much practice is required.

II. Participant Open-Ended Observation (Technique 12)

Participant open-ended observation refers to a situation in which the observer partakes in the classroom activities. The observer may assist in the instruction by working with a group or helping individual students.

The observer may take notes or just jot down some ideas for later recall. The advantage of having the observer "participate" in the class is that many insights may be culled from direct participation that might otherwise be missed from detached observations.

The types of observation possible are similar to detached open-ended narratives. Using this procedure, the observer either makes notes during the activities or simply summarizes events after the observation period. The essential element here is that the observer is in a unique position to better understand classroom interactions because he or she is actively involved.

Observers should feel free to vary their approaches (detached or participant), depending on a given situation. Sometimes, for example, a teacher may feel uncomfortable having the supervisor participate, explaining that it may be distracting. I highly suggest arranging the format of observation with the teacher in advance.

Practice participant open-ended observation as you did previously with the detached open-ended narrative.

III. Child-Centered Learning Observation (Technique 13)

Based on constructivist learning theory, *child-centered learning observation* focuses primarily on the learner, the student, rather than on the instructor. By incorporating a qualitative approach (detached or participatory), the observer may record observations in response to these and other learner-centered questions:

- Were the children learning/thinking?
- What kinds of questions were being asked (e.g., open ended)?
- How were children treated?
- What opportunities were provided for children to learn in different ways?
- Who is the source of knowledge?

- Were kids talking to kids?
- Were children designing their own learning?
- Who assesses learning?
- What did we learn about the children?

Child-centered learning observations provide invaluable insights into student learning that would otherwise be overlooked by focusing only on the teacher. They also allow the teacher to reflect on the causes of the student's behavior or response, which may have originated in the teacher's interaction with the student.

IV. Nonverbal Techniques (Technique 14)

Materials. Nonverbal observation chart (see, e.g., Table 3.10)

Explanation. Observations are collaboratively arranged and made in a series of short visits at various times during one day or over several days. Although a

Table 3.10   An Observation Chart

Nonverbal Technique	*Anecdotal Observations*
Proxemics	
Standing near student(s)	
Moving toward student(s)	
Touching student(s)	
Moving about room	
Kinesics	
Eye contact	
Touching	
Smiling	
Nodding affirmatively	
Open arm movements	
Frowning	
Stern look	
Finger to lips	
Pointing	
Arms crossed	
Hand on hips	
Prosody	
Varies voice tone	
Varies pitch	
Varies rhythm	
Immediacy	
Responds with warmth	

checklist can be used noting each time the teacher uses a particular nonverbal technique, we prefer the observer to keep a running record of the types of nonverbal interactions used along with annotations describing the nature and impact of those interventions.

Proxemics is the teacher's use of perception and space. The closer a teacher is to a student, the less likely the student is to behave inappropriately. For example, the teacher may stand near or move toward a potentially disruptive student as a behavior control strategy. This technique works best with teachers who customarily stand and move about. Another use of proxemics is to arrange classroom furniture in such a way as to convey warmth and closeness.

Kinesics is the teacher's use of facial and body cues, such as smiling, frowning, staring, pointing, or hands on hips. These cues communicate strong messages, work well from a distance, and help signal individuals and groups when they are disrupting others. Kinesic cues should be considered as an aid to conventional classroom management methods. The best way to learn these cues is to practice them with others and in front of a mirror.

Prosody is concerned with tone, pitch, and rhythm of the teacher's voice and communicates the importance of what is being said. Teachers who use this tool know that yelling and high-pitched voices tend to excite rather than calm students. Effective use of prosody can convey caring, empathy, and warmth as well as a love of teaching and students.

Immediacy is the degree of perceived or psychological closeness between people. Teachers who use this technique are physically close to students, use socially appropriate touching, exhibit warmth, and use open body postures while communicating. For example, lightly touching a student's shoulder or upper arm while explaining an assignment tells that student the teacher cares and wants him or her to be successful.

SUMMARY OF OBSERVATION TOOLS

I have described two approaches to observation: quantitative and qualitative. A total of fourteen techniques were reviewed and practiced. I have not included videotaping and audio recording as separate tools; rather, they are valuable instruments that can be used with any of the tools and techniques described in this chapter. According to Acheson and Gall (1997), "Video and audio recordings are among the most objective observation techniques. . . . They allow teachers to see themselves as students see them. . . . [They] can pick up a great deal of what teachers and students are doing and saying. A good recording captures the 'feel' of classroom interaction" (p. 111).

Videos and audios, according to Acheson and Gall, are examples of "wide lenses" that are particularly useful "in supervising teachers who are defensive or who are not yet ready to select particular teaching behaviors for improvement" (p. 107). Acheson and Gall conclude, "After reviewing wide-lens data, these teachers may be more ready to reflect on their teaching, identify specific teaching behaviors for focused observations, and set self-improvement goals" (pp. 107–108).

Research demonstrates that teachers are likely to change their instructional behaviors on their own after their classroom has been described to them by an observer. Observation is a mirror and thus a stimulus for change. Good supervision is about engaging teachers in reflective thinking and discussion based on insightful and useful observation tools and techniques. In the next chapter, we place these observation tools within the context of a clinical supervision program.

Clinical Supervision Step 3: The Postconference

Often eliminated, this final step is critical. Find time for this important follow-up session. If you really want to serve as an instructional leader you will make time for this important activity. Without it, the previous two steps are nearly worthless. Teacher confidence will wane without adequate follow-up. As you begin the postconference, ask the teacher how she or he felt about the lesson. Adhere to the three following approaches, depending on the developmental level of the teacher.

Key Steps—Directive Informational Approach

1. *Identify the problem or goal and solicit clarifying information.*

2. *Offer solutions. Ask for the teacher's input into the alternatives offered and request additional ideas.*

3. *Summarize chosen alternatives, ask for confirmation, and request that the teacher restate final choices.*

4. *Set a follow-up plan and meeting.*

Key Steps—Collaborative Approach

1. *Identify the problem from the teacher's perspective, soliciting as much clarifying information as possible.*

2. *Reflect back what you've heard for accuracy.*

3. *Begin collaborative brainstorming, asking the teacher for his or her ideas first.*

4. *Problem solve through a sharing and discussion of options.*

5. *Agree on a plan and follow-up meeting.*

Key Steps—Self-Directed Approach

1. *Listen carefully to the teacher's initial statement.*

2. *Reflect back your understanding of the problem.*

3. *Constantly clarify and reflect until the real problem is identified.*

4. *Have the teacher problem solve and explore consequences of various actions.*

5. *The teacher commits to a decision and firms up a plan.*

6. *The supervisor restates the teacher's plan and sets a follow-up meeting.*

REFLECT

Find a colleague with whom you can practice the three steps of clinical supervision. You play the role of the AP and set up any scenario: for example, you are observing a history lesson at the high school level for 20 minutes. Complete the clinical supervision cycle and prepare the following written report:

A. Summarize or recount each phase of the cycle: planning conference, observation, and postconference.

B. Analyze the data from each approach choice you made and then interpret the data.

  1. How much teacher input was there in the planning conference? Would you recommend a change in the approach to this teacher in another planning session? Why?

2. Did the observation tool reveal the behaviors on which you and your colleague agreed to focus? How or why not? Was the observation tool you chose appropriate and effective? Is it a tool you would use again? Why or why not?

3. What were the teacher's reactions to the process?

C. Provide a final reflection on the whole process, that is, your personal evaluation of what worked and was of value, and what you will think about doing differently in the future.

_____

_____

_____

_____

CONCLUSION

This chapter has introduced us to the cycle of clinical supervision. The cycle presented consists of three basic stages:

1. The planning conference

2. The observation

3. The postconference

An important topic not discussed is how to implement such practice. A final word on this point is in order. First, you as AP should feel secure in implementing the clinical supervision cycle. Second, obtaining support from your principal is essential. With such support, you must organize your time to allow for all clinical supervision steps. The bottom line is that if you value the benefits of clinical supervision to promote instructional dialogue with teachers about teaching and learning then you'll find the time.

IN-BASKET SIMULATION

1. You are a newly assigned AP in a K–6 elementary school. During informal observations of science lessons you find teachers are using whole-class instruction as the primary instructional strategy. You also notice few teachers using experiments that are student initiated and conducted. You notice that students are bored and off task. What specific suggestions would you give the teachers? Describe your entire approach and explain how you might incorporate clinical supervisory practices. (Answers may vary. Select one of the three approaches explained in this chapter. Remember to select an approach matched to the developmental level of the particular teacher. Compare your responses to information presented earlier in the chapter.)

2. Your principal supports your efforts as an instructional leader at the high school level. He is an administrator type, not an instructional leader. Your faculty are used to the traditional method of evaluation. How would you establish a culture supportive of clinical practice? Be specific. (Here are some suggested solutions: Begin small by collaborating with a like-minded and receptive teacher or two about your ideas; field-test your ideas with them [the word will spread that it works—of course, first obtain principal approval]; conduct a demonstration lesson; invite a teacher or two to visit another school where the cycle works; etc.)

4

Instructional
Improvement

*Insufficient attention has been given to APs, that APs want more active
involvement in instructional and leadership matters.*

—Jeffrey Glanz, "Redefining the
Roles and Responsibilities of Assistant Principals"

◆

FOCUS QUESTIONS

1. Do you consider yourself a teacher of teachers? Explain.

2. Why is instructional leadership the most important task/responsibility of APs?

3. What do you need to know to serve as an effective instructional leader?

4. How will you make time for instructional leadership as an AP?

5. What do teachers need to do to promote student achievement?

6. How do you intend to promote instructional improvement?

If the AP is to gain credibility, respectability, and a degree of professionalism in terms of curricular and instructional responsibility then he or she must be expertly trained in these areas and must truly be perceived as a teacher of teachers. An AP therefore must demonstrate not only good pedagogical skills but also the ability to communicate and coordinate approaches that encourage better teaching in others. APs as instructional leaders must establish a culture that focuses on instruction as the number one priority on a grade level or in a school. APs as instructional leaders incorporate supervision, staff development, action research, and curriculum development in an overall plan to promote instructional improvement.

Among the leading researchers in the field of instructional leadership are Jo Blasé and Joseph Blasé (1998). Their *Handbook of Instructional Leadership* outlines what good principals do to promote teaching and learning. Although they speak of principals, their insights apply as well to APs charged with promoting instructional improvement. Good instructional leaders, according to these authors, conduct meaningful and ongoing instructional conferences, provide relevant and continuous staff development, and encourage teacher reflection about their own teaching practice. Blasé and Blasé identify specific supervisor behaviors that encourage meaningful conferences. Such behaviors include making suggestions, giving feedback, modeling best practice, using inquiry, and soliciting advice and opinions from teachers. Behaviors associated with providing staff development include developing coaching relationships and using action research, as well as others. Good supervisors develop teacher reflection through classroom observation, dialogue, suggestion, and praise.

Blasé and Blasé (1998) conclude their comprehensive study by offering the following suggestions that promote instructional improvement:

• Talk openly and frequently about instruction. Good APs will make time to discuss teaching and learning. Grade conferences, e-mails, and other correspondence will focus on instruction. Developing a climate that encourages the exchange of ideas about teaching and learning is critical (McEwan, 2003).

• Provide time and peer connections for teachers. Good APs understand that teachers learn from each other. Rarely do teachers have the time to observe other teachers practice the art of teaching. APs can provide for intervisitations by releasing teachers from time to time to observe each other and to share reflections about good teaching practice. APs may at times release teachers to visit other exemplary teachers in other schools or attend local, state, or national education conferences (Blasé & Blasé, 2002).

• Empower teachers. Fostering collaborative decision making, professional growth opportunities for teachers, and autonomous behavior among teachers go a long way to making teachers feel like professional educators (Blasé & Blasé, 1998).

- Understand and embrace the challenges of change. Encouraging teachers to take instructional risks is a mark of a good instructional leader (Fullan, 1995).

- Lead. Good APs realize that all teachers are leaders in their own right and provide for leadership opportunities such as conducting instructional workshops and conferences (Glanz, 2003).

RECOLLECTION

I recall my first several years of teaching in an urban elementary school. The principal had an excellent reputation as an administrator. He was well organized, prompt, and efficient. He prided himself on his meticulous reports that were distributed to officials in the district office. He was not, however, an instructional leader.

He taught for about four years before assuming his first administrative position as an assistant principal. Within a few years he was promoted to principal. His organizational and interpersonal skills brought him notoriety. I recall that he was an avid runner. Although he didn't run marathons, he was adept at LSD, that is, long slow distance runs. We shared many a conversation about running, because at the time I too was into LSD. We usually conversed about aspects of running from the shoes we wore to where we ran. These conversations took place while waiting to take my class up to the classroom during morning lineup. We never spoke about teaching or about what I was doing to promote student achievement.

The principal did not feel comfortable talking about teaching. After all, he had only been a teacher for a short time. His forte was administration. He believed that a good principal sets a conducive tone in a school building so as to allow teachers to "do their thing," as he used to say back in the 1970s. His philosophy was to foster good student discipline, provide a well-run school, and leave instruction to teachers.

As a new teacher, I yearned to talk to someone about my instructional practices. Although the district reading supervisor occasionally popped in, our conversations were usually brief. Usually I had to learn through trial and error. Those poor kids during my early years of teaching were victims of my instructional experiments.

It was only several years later when I was transferred into another school in another district that I realized how valuable a supervisor can be as instructional leader. Mr. Chiradelli, our AP, was not only well organized and personable but also comfortable with talking to us about teaching. He was the first AP

(Continued)

(Continued)

who actually said to me, "Jeffrey, no, let me show you." On the spot, he demonstrated good pedagogical practice by taking over my class to show me how to more effectively pose critical thinking questions. Seeing a model in action, I was uplifted. Mr. Chiradelli was a teacher of teachers and a very effective AP.

RESPOND

Charlotte Danielson, in a 1996 work titled *Enhancing Professional Practice: A Framework for Teaching* published by the Association for Supervision and Curriculum Development (see Resource A), developed a framework or model for understanding teaching based on current research in the field. She identified "components" clustered into four domains of teaching responsibility: planning and preparation, classroom environment, instruction, and professional responsibilities. I developed and adapted the following questionnaire based on her framework. Please take the survey now because it will *serve as an important reflective tool to judge what you consider as instructionally important.* Please note that your responses are private. Therefore, your honest responses to the various items below will best *serve as reflective tools to assist you in becoming an even better instructional leader.*

Analyzing Your Responses

Note that the items draw from research that highlights good educational practice. Review your responses and circle responses that concern you. For instance, if you circled Strongly Agree for "I am rarely alert to teacher's instructional needs," ask yourself, "Why is this is a problem?" "How can I remedy the situation?" and "What additional resources or assistance might I need?" If you agree, share and compare responses with another educator. The dialogue that will ensue will serve as a helpful vehicle to move toward more effective practice.

In summary, review your responses for each of the four domains as noted in the following discussion:

Domain 1: Planning and preparation. This domain demonstrates your comfort level in working with teachers on content and pedagogical knowledge,

Form 4.1   Respond

<table>
<tr><td colspan="5">Article I. RESPOND</td></tr>
<tr><td>SA = Strongly Agree ("For the most part, yes")
A = Agree ("Yes, but . . .")
D = Disagree ("No, but . . .")
SD = Strongly Disagree ("For the most part, no")</td><td>SA</td><td>A</td><td>D</td><td>SD</td></tr>
<tr><td>Planning and Preparation</td><td></td><td></td><td></td><td></td></tr>
<tr><td>1. Teachers should be offered guidance in planning and preparing for instruction, and I feel comfortable doing so.</td><td></td><td></td><td></td><td></td></tr>
<tr><td>2. Good teachers should display solid content knowledge and make connections with the parts of their discipline or with other disciplines.</td><td></td><td></td><td></td><td></td></tr>
<tr><td>3. Good teachers should consider the importance of prerequisite knowledge when introducing new topics.</td><td></td><td></td><td></td><td></td></tr>
<tr><td>4. Good teachers actively build on students' prior knowledge and seek causes for students' misunderstanding.</td><td></td><td></td><td></td><td></td></tr>
<tr><td>5. Good teachers are content knowledgeable, but may need additional assistance with pedagogical strategies and techniques, and I feel comfortable providing such assistance.</td><td></td><td></td><td></td><td></td></tr>
<tr><td>6. I am familiar with pedagogical strategies and continually search for the best practices to share with my teachers.</td><td></td><td></td><td></td><td></td></tr>
<tr><td>7. Good teachers know much about the developmental needs of their students.</td><td></td><td></td><td></td><td></td></tr>
<tr><td>8. APs are familiar with learning styles and multiple intelligences theories and can help teachers apply them to instructional practice.</td><td></td><td></td><td></td><td></td></tr>
<tr><td>9. I do not fully recognize the value of understanding teachers' skills and knowledge as a basis for their teaching.</td><td></td><td></td><td></td><td></td></tr>
<tr><td>10. Goal setting is critical to teacher success in planning and preparing, and the AP should offer to collaborate with teachers in this area.</td><td></td><td></td><td></td><td></td></tr>
<tr><td>11. I am familiar with curricular and teaching resources to assist teachers.</td><td></td><td></td><td></td><td></td></tr>
</table>

(Continued)

Form 4.1 (Continued)

12. I know I can help teachers develop appropriate learning activities suitable for students.				
13. I can help teachers plan for a variety of meaningful learning activities matched to school/district/state instructional goals.				
14. I would encourage teachers to use varied instructional grouping.				
15. I can assist teachers in developing a systematic plan for assessment of student learning.				
16. I can provide professional development for teachers in planning and preparation.				
The Classroom Environment				
1. I realize the importance of classroom management and discipline.				
2. I expect that teacher interactions with students are generally friendly and demonstrate warmth and caring.				
3. I expect teachers to develop a system of discipline without my assistance.				
4. I will play an active role in monitoring grade/school discipline plans.				
5. I support the classroom teachers in matters of discipline.				
6. I always communicate high expectations to all my teachers that they are the critical element in the classroom.				
7. I expect teachers to have a well-established and well-defined system of rules and procedures.				
8. I expect that teachers are alert to student behavior at all times.				
9. I can provide professional development to teachers on classroom management.				
10. As a teacher, I was a competent classroom manager.				
Instruction				
1. I expect that teachers' directions to students are clear and not confusing.				

2. My directives to teachers about instruction are clear.				
3. My spoken language as a teacher was clear and appropriate to the grade level of my students.				
4. I believe that teacher questioning techniques are among the most critical skills needed to promote pupil learning, and I feel comfortable in helping teachers frame good questions.				
5. Teacher questions must be uniformly of high quality.				
6. From my experience, teachers mostly lecture (talk) to students without enough student participation.				
7. I encourage teachers to encourage students to participate and prefer for students to take an active role in learning.				
8. I can provide a workshop for teachers on giving assignments that are appropriate to students and that engage students mentally.				
9. I don't know how to group students appropriately for instruction.				
10. I am very familiar with grouping strategies to promote instruction.				
11. I can advise teachers on how best to select appropriate and effective instructional materials and resources.				
12. My demo lessons to teachers are highly coherent, and my pacing is consistent and appropriate.				
13. I rarely provide appropriate feedback to my teachers.				
14. Feedback to my teachers is consistent, appropriate, and of high quality.				
15. I expect my teachers to rely heavily on the teacher's manual for instruction.				
16. I consistently encourage teachers to seek my advice on teaching and learning matters.				
17. I encourage teachers to use wait time effectively.				

(Continued)

Form 4.1 (Continued)

18. I feel competent enough to give a workshop to teachers on effective use of wait time.				
19. I consider myself an instructional leader.				
20. Teachers perceive me as an instructional leader.				
Professional Responsibilities				
1. I have difficulty assessing the effectiveness of teachers.				
2. I can accurately assess how well I am doing as an instructional leader.				
3. I really don't know how to improve teaching skills.				
4. I am aware of what I need to do in order to become an effective instructional leader.				
5. I rarely encourage parents to become involved in instructional matters.				
6. I actively and consistently invite parents to visit classrooms.				
7. I feel comfortable giving workshops to parents on curricular and/or instructional matters.				
8. I have difficulty relating to my colleagues in a cordial and professional manner.				
9. I collaborate with my colleagues in a cordial and professional manner.				
10. I avoid becoming involved in school and district projects.				
11. I rarely encourage teachers to seek to engage in professional development activities.				
12. I seek out opportunities for professional development to enhance my pedagogical skills.				
13. I am rarely alert to teachers' instructional needs.				
14. I serve teachers.				
15. I am an advocate for student's rights.				
16. I am an advocate for teacher's rights.				
17. I rarely encourage teachers to serve on a school-based committee.				
18. I enjoy working with teachers collaboratively on instructional matters.				

knowledge of students and resources, ability to select instructional goals, and the degree to which you help them assess learning.

SA A D SD 1. My ability to work with teachers on planning and preparation are satisfactory.

Domain 2: The classroom environment. This domain assesses the degree to which you encourage and create an environment of respect and caring and establish a culture for learning related to many aspects of classroom environment.

SA A D SD 2. I am satisfied that my ability to work with teachers on the classroom environment is satisfactory.

Domain 3: Instruction. This domain assesses the ability to work with teachers to communicate with clarity, use questioning and discussion techniques, engage students in learning, provide feedback to students, and demonstrate flexibility and responsiveness to students' instructional needs.

SA A D SD 3. I am satisfied that my knowledge and skills of instruction are satisfactory.

Domain 4: Professional responsibilities. This domain assesses the degree to which you encourage teachers to reflect on teaching, maintain accurate records, communicate with parents, contribute to the school or district, grow and develop professionally, and show professionalism.

SA A D SD 4. I am satisfied that I am professionally responsible.

The remainder of this chapter is devoted to the following points:

- Introducing a mnemonic (PCOWBIRDS) that includes information that is useful in addressing and promoting instructional matters
- Reviewing key components in lesson planning and delivery, the heart of any instructional program
- Discussing how to make time for instructional matters

Promoting Instruction

Supervision

Supervision is a dynamic, ongoing, and collaborative process that involves strategies to enhance instructional improvement. An educational leader is concerned with facilitating an environment conducive to learning (Sullivan & Glanz, 2004).

A competent instructional leader should attend to **PCOWBIRDS***!*

P = *Plans:* Planning is integral to instructional success, and the AP as an educational leader should help a teacher develop appropriate and meaningful instructional activities and learning experiences. Checking plans, offering suggestions, coplanning, reviewing procedures, and framing thought-provoking questions, among other important aspects, are essential. Supervision, then, involves assisting teachers to better plan their lessons and units of instruction. See the next section of this chapter that addresses aspects of lesson planning and delivery in more detail. Also, see Chapter 3 for a discussion of planning in relation to the clinical supervision process.

C = *Conferences:* Conferencing with teachers, formally and informally, in order to share ideas and develop alternate instructional strategies is an essential supervisory responsibility. Meeting and talking with teachers throughout the day and school year on instructional matters are essential. Your focus as an instructional leader must be on teaching and learning. Sharing insights, reviewing recent research (Marzano, Pickering, & Pollock, 2001), and engaging in reflective practice are very important. Formal and informal conferencing must be continuous and should involve teachers in the planning and agenda of conferences. The key to establishing a grade or school culture that fosters instructional dialogue for the purpose of improving teaching and learning is to consider such an activity your number one priority and, thus, to devote time and energies to ensuring and nurturing it.

O = *Observations:* An educational leader should offer her or his expertise by both formally and informally observing classroom interaction. A skilled AP who utilizes various observation systems (e.g., Acheson & Gall, 1997; Glickman, Gordon, & Ross-Gordon, 2004; Sullivan & Glanz, 2004) can facilitate instructional improvement by documenting classroom interaction so that a teacher might reflect upon and react to what has been observed. Providing teachers with evidence of classroom interaction is fundamental to begin helping them understand what they are doing or not doing to promote student learning. Observations play a key role in supervision. As Yogi Berra once quipped, "You can observe a lot by watching." Consult Sullivan and Glanz (2004) for many quantitative and qualitative observation tools.

W = *Workshops:* APs as educational leaders should conduct or organize various workshops for teachers on relevant instructional topics such as cooperative learning, alternative teaching strategies, and multiple intelligences. Sometimes APs will feel comfortable in conducting a workshop. APs are not expected, of course, to be conversant in all areas. Sometimes they may ask an outside consultant or expert in a particular field to conduct a workshop on a topic of interest to teachers or even ask one of the more experienced teachers to do so. The bottom line here is that you, as AP, realize the importance of instruction as the main focus of your work. Realizing the importance of instruction, you plan and coordinate varied and continuous workshops for teachers. These workshops may be conducted as a part of professional development days designated by the school or district, as part of a grade or faculty conference, or as an after/before school or even summer activity.

B = *Bulletins:* Bulletins, journals, reports, and newsletters can be disseminated to interested faculty. One of my teachers became interested in cooperative learning after attending a reading conference. I sustained her interest by placing several articles about cooperative learning in her mailbox. APs are conversant with the literature of various fields and subscribe to various journals including *Educational Leadership, Kappan, Journal of Curriculum and Supervision, Elementary School Journal, Instructor, Teaching K-12, Journal of Learning Disabilities,* and others. APs are always on the alert for relevant articles, bulletins, and publications that encourage and support instructional improvement.

I = *Intervisitations:* Teachers rarely have the opportunity to visit and observe colleagues. An AP can facilitate intervisitations by rearranging the schedule so that teachers might observe one another and then share common instructional strategies or discuss common problems. Intervisitations, to be effective, must be voluntary and nonjudgmental. Shared dialogue about instructional practices goes a long way toward promoting instructional improvement.

R = *Resources:* APs should make available for teachers a variety of instructional materials and technologies to enhance instructional improvement. Purchasing textbooks, trade books, computers, LCD projectors, and other relevant resources is important to support an instructional program.

D = *Demonstration lessons:* An AP presumably is a teacher of teachers. An AP is not necessarily the foremost teacher in a school, but she or he should feel comfortable in providing "demo" lessons for teachers, when appropriate. Providing such lessons enhances supervisory credibility among teachers and provides instructional support.

Parenthetically, I once noticed during a formal observation that the teacher was not using wait time effectively. He posed good questions, but waited only about 2 seconds before calling on someone. As his AP, I suggested that he watch me teach a lesson and notice how long I wait after posing a question before calling on a pupil. These observations were the basis for a follow-up conference at which we discussed the research on "wait time" and the advantages of waiting before calling on a pupil. As the saying goes, "a picture is worth a thousand words." Having this particular teacher watch me demonstrate effective use of wait time was more valuable than had I merely told him what to do. Competent supervisors not only suggest how to do something, they also must "demonstrate" how it should be done.

S = *Staff development:* APs can aid instructional improvement by providing staff development that is "purposeful and articulated," "participatory and collaborative," "knowledge-based," "ongoing," "developmental," and "analytic and reflective" (Griffin, 1997). Although I addressed workshops earlier, staff development means a series of collaboratively planned and implemented workshops on single or varied topics over time. Understanding the relationship between staff development and instructional improvement is critical. Teachers need continued and sustained instructional support. A good AP will plan for such meaningful staff development.

So, as you strive to promote instructional improvement keep in mind PCOWBIRDS.

REFLECT

How might PCOWBIRDS serve as a useful mnemonic to help you develop and maintain an instructional emphasis in your work?

_____

_____

_____

_____

Lesson Planning

The information in this section is very basic. APs know this information quite well. I am not necessarily including this information for a review, but perhaps readers can cull from it material to be used with faculty, especially new teachers, in a workshop or two. Feel free to photocopy any of this information to be read and reviewed by your faculty.

Here's an evaluation letter I presented to one of the fourth grade teachers I observed when I served as AP in a K–5 urban school:

Dear Ms. Xavier:

I requested to observe you teaching a lesson in Basal Reading. At our preobservation conference, you provided me with a detailed written lesson plan. Upon observing your lesson, I noted the following positive features:

1. I was impressed with this well-organized and well-planned lesson. The aim was clearly written on the board, "How do we sum up important information?" The students were reading a story titled, "Memories" in the *Over the Moon* reader. You also noted that your instructional standards tied to the state learning standards.

2. You began the lesson by asking, "What are ways we sum up information?" You elicited various responses such as titles, illustrations, telegrams, headlines, graphs, and book reports. You then reviewed key vocabulary words and had students skim the story. This lesson contained many good elements from silent and oral reading to good provocative questions and summaries. The lesson was quite comprehensive. The pupils were attentive and well mannered.

Although the lesson was fine, please consider the following few suggestions for improvement, as we discussed at our postobservation conference:

• Utilize wait time: Wait time is an instructional strategy that refers to the amount of time students have to think during questioning. Research indicates that providing between 7 and 10 seconds for students to think before the teacher answers a question or calls on someone else improves student accurate participation.

• Check for understanding: Although you have definitely established a warm, friendly, and supportive classroom environment conducive to eliciting student participation, research indicates that when teachers proactively check students' understanding, retention of difficult subject matter increases dramatically. Calling on students who do not volunteer a response and/or having them repeat content information in their own words out loud or to a neighboring student increases likelihood that students really understand the material.

• Use focused questions: We discussed that use of one well-focused question (which you developed quite well) should suffice, under normal circumstances, to stimulate thought and participation. Use of multiple questions to get across the same idea may, at times, not be necessary.

Thank you for the wonderful opportunity to observe you teach. Please invite me again in the near future.

I am not presenting this observation/evaluation report as a model, but rather to indicate a number of issues. First, a well-planned lesson is critical for effective teaching. Planning is the first stage in a three-stage process that also includes implementing the lesson and evaluating the lesson. In this evaluation report an outside observer (i.e., supervisor) conducted the traditional evaluation. More often, teachers themselves can determine whether or not a particular lesson was effective. Parenthetically, formal evaluation yields little change in teaching behavior, in my estimation. If instructional improvement is to occur, then the evaluative mode has to be removed from the process. Evaluation, however, does have its place to ensure accountability and to ensure that the teacher in front of the class is competent. Aside from that narrow function, evaluation should give way to activities that really promote instructional improvement such as peer coaching (teachers assisting teachers) or clinical supervision (observations for feedback devoid of evaluation; see Chapter 3).

A second point to be gleaned from the earlier report is that lesson planning and writing are not only done when a teacher is formally observed. Lesson planning is an ongoing, introspective process that engages the teacher in selecting the most appropriate learning objectives and activities for a particular class. All teachers, regardless of experience, need to plan, and planning occurs before, during, and after instruction.

In this section of the chapter, I will highlight important elements that go into an effective lesson. Professional development opportunities can be developed to help teachers improve their lessons. As information is presented in the following section, try to think of ways to incorporate them to help teachers improve teaching and promote student learning.

Lesson planning—the term suggests many different connotations. So many teachers would say that it implies a necessary but unpleasant chore. Others might describe it as burdensome paperwork, an outline for instruction, or even a helpful guide. No matter whether required or not, no matter whether written elaborately or briefly, lesson plans are a part of all teachers' weekly tasks. Without a plan, instruction becomes a random assortment of activities with little rhyme or reason.

Lesson planning is usually associated with only a written design developed by the teacher. Actually, it involves two activities:

1. Mental planning

2. The written plan book

In mental planning, teachers consider questions, reflect on the topic, and envision what might occur in subsequent lessons. Mental planning is an important and legitimate prerequisite for the written plan. It takes into consideration such things as the textbook, a list of prescribed skills, curriculum standards, library materials, and so on. It is not unlike the mental preparation of an athlete, who begins by envisioning a successful shot, for instance. Teachers also need to envision what their lesson will accomplish, what they want students to learn and know at the end, and how they will go about achieving their objectives.

The written plan book is a shorthand outline of what will develop in the classroom based on the mental planning. The written plan serves as a reminder of topics, concepts, skills, and activities that the teacher wants to be sure to use at some point. Basically, it's the teacher's road map. Different schools will require different plan books and plans. This chapter merely highlights the main parts of a lesson.

Lesson plans are most effective when the interrelationships of skills are fostered. Most of us can agree with the premise that schooling should offer children opportunities to make connections, to think, and to expand learning. It is false to assume that just because students learn various skills, they will automatically know how to use them in relationships. It is also false to assume that texts make the connections for us. Some textbooks do only a fair job in structuring for continuity. Thus it becomes the teacher's responsibility to develop lessons that expand thinking and interrelate skills. For example, teachers can develop reading lessons that help students to learn that punctuation, context, and phonics clues all work together to interpret the written word. Subjects such as science, reading, and social studies can be interrelated. For example, a story about Columbus can be related to map reading skills taught in social studies and to navigation by constellations in science. Children need to be encouraged to make connections between various lessons, between subjects, and between in-school and out-of-school life.

Another good practice is to develop long-range as well as short-range goals. Having long-range goals (monthly, quarterly, or yearly) helps teachers maintain an overall perspective and helps to serve as a guide for day-to-day instruction.

It is very important to use teacher judgment when writing short-range objectives. Some subject objectives and daily plans, such as reading and mathematics, are greatly influenced by texts. Texts do not always provide the continuity necessary for effective learning. Also, text suggestions often need to be modified to fit individual classroom situations. Teachers should make changes in textbook guides based on criteria such as the following:

- Do these students already know this material? Does it need reviewing?
- Will this activity fit into the amount of time I have?
- How can I relate to what the students know?
- Could I do part of this activity as independent work for the group to complete while I work with another group?

When determining objectives and writing lesson plans, teachers should consider students' learning styles. Some students are fast, others slow; some are easily motivated, others difficult to motivate; some do well in large groups, others in small groups; some do better with written work, others with oral work. By taking such learning characteristics into consideration, teachers can develop strategies that are appropriate for various classes.

It is a good habit to include the method of evaluation. The primary purpose of testing is to determine the extent of student mastery of the objectives, not to determine grades. For any lesson to be productive, teachers must receive feedback as to how well the objectives are being met. To receive useful feedback, teachers should spend sufficient time incorporating good evaluation measures as part of lesson planning.

Some other helpful points for effective daily plans include the following:

- Estimate the time required for various activities; plan enough—don't get caught short (students are more apt to get in trouble when they have too much free time on their hands); have additional activities in reserve for those occasions when your regular lessons are completed early.
- Jot down any changes you would like to make for future use while it is fresh in your mind.
- Check off items as they are completed.
- Be flexible and make adjustments as you go. (Teachers know best how to adjust their lesson plans based on evaluations of students' progress. Sometimes teachers need to move more slowly and give more instruction before proceeding to new objectives.)

The actual format of lesson plans is not as important as the process of developing the plans. Teachers should use whatever format is most workable as long as it is clear and easy to follow (unless, of course, you, the AP, require them to use a certain format). As implied by the points already described, teachers should consider using the following process when writing lesson plans:

1. Analyze students' learning styles.

2. Specify long-range goals (monthly, quarterly, or yearly). These long-range goals should determine daily lesson plans.

3. Specify objectives. Keep in mind the interrelationship in instruction.

4. Select or design activities and materials.

5. Include how students will be tested to determine the effectiveness of instruction.

6. Evaluate activities and make revisions as necessary.

No matter whether teacher planning is detailed or general, it is important. It helps teachers to organize their thoughts, meet objectives, coordinate materials, and be prepared for instruction. By planning properly, teaching will be more effective.

ESSENTIAL COMPONENTS AND CRITERIA OF A SUCCESSFUL LESSON

Again, this subsection can actually be photocopied and used with first-year teachers, for instance, as a review for discussion during a faculty or grade meeting or workshop.

Aim and Objectives

1. Meaningful and appropriate to the levels of students

2. Elicited from students

3. Personalized in question form

4. Definite and expressed

5. Achieved and realized

6. Written on board and in student's notebook

7. Varied using Bloom's Taxonomy (see the following)

Decide what your goals are in teaching this unit. In looking over the content that you plan to teach in a lesson, you must ask the question "What do I want the pupils to derive from the lesson that will be meaningful and worthwhile?" The aim that you decide upon will be the backbone of the lesson. All activities should point toward the achievement of that aim. Let the student derive the aim rather than having the teacher state it at the outset. This helps the students identify with the lesson and make it their own. Your motivation should be the vehicle for revealing the aim to the class. The objectives do not necessarily have to be formally stated. Rather, they are written explicitly in your plan book. The aim is a general statement based on your objectives. Some teachers prefer to inform students about both the aim and the objectives. See Resource B.

Motivation

1. Aroused interest

2. Sustained interest

3. Connected to aim of lesson

4. Challenged students

5. Related to students' experiences

6. Easy transition to lesson

Motivation is a device to arouse student interest in the content to be taught, and also to reveal to the class the aim of the lesson. Effective motivations stimulate curiosity and utilize the experiences and the knowledge of the pupils. Some devices that can be used to motivate a lesson are challenging statements, personal experiences, cartoons, a problem, a chart, or an anecdote. Some call this stage "anticipatory sets."

Questions

1. Well phrased and understood

2. Stimulated critical thinking

3. Well distributed among students in class

4. Check for understanding

Pitfalls in Questioning

1. Calling on student first and then asking question

2. Relying only on volunteers

3. Repeating students' responses to questions

4. Saying "tell me," not "us"

5. Framing multiple questions

Student Responses

1. Avoid choral responses

2. Don't repeat student response

3. Use praise, prompt (if student answers incorrectly), probe (if student answers correctly but lacks depth) techniques

Aside from developing your aim and learning objectives, your use of questions is the most critical part of your lesson. The success or failure of a lesson is largely determined by the questioning techniques employed, by the quality of the questions, and by the sequence in which the questions are asked. Questioning is a powerful teaching tool. Through questioning, you can develop student learning styles and habits, stimulate higher levels of thinking, foster new learning, and evaluate the progress of achievement. You actually can mold students' minds through the effective use of questions.

Unfortunately, we often do not make as effective use of questions as we could, and as we should. Research has shown that most teacher questions are on the lower levels of thinking, predominantly information and short answers, rather than on the higher levels, such as judgment, inference, application, analysis, and synthesis. This problem can be overcome by becoming familiar with the thinking hierarchy (such as Bloom's Taxonomy) and by generating questions that promote higher thinking.

Benjamin Bloom's taxonomy is one of the most important concepts in all of teaching. Basically, he asserts that learning occurs in a hierarchical manner, beginning with simple thinking processes and proceeding step by step through more complex processes. He classifies six major learning behaviors, or ways of thinking, that translate into six types of questions that you need to consider and use appropriately:

1. Knowledge—The lowest, most basic level of learning or thinking occurs when students are asked to recall or recognize bits of information. Key words here are *who, what, when, which, how many, name, identify, recall,* and so on. Examples include "Who discovered the Indian Ocean?" "What happened to Alice in the story?" "Where did her mother send her?" and so on. Students merely are asked to recall bits of information. At this stage, students may simply memorize information but may not comprehend what they have learned. I once had a fourth grader who had phenomenal decoding skills who could read every word in the *New York Times*. Everyone marveled at his ability to "read." He really couldn't read because he could not *understand* what he had read, which brings us to Bloom's second and higher level.

2. Comprehension—This next behavior or thinking level occurs when students are able to explain or paraphrase information. Asking students to explain in their own words what a concept means or to give an example may indicate that students comprehend the information. Key words here are *describe, explain, use your own words, translate, interpret,* and so on. Examples include "What do the words . . . mean?" "Explain what . . . means," and so on. Ask a student, "What is a Lut?" He doesn't know, so you tell him, "A Lut is a Zut." Now, you ask him again, "Okay, what is a Lut?" He responds, "It's a Zut." Although he has some

knowledge, that is, that a Lut is a Zut, he may not understand what a Lut really is. Ask, "Okay, explain in your own words what a Lut is? Zut?" If he is able to explain correctly, you may assume he comprehends the information.

3. Application—This next higher level of thinking or behavior requires the student to use the information learned to solve a specific problem or apply it to a situation. Key words here are *solve, choose, apply,* and so on. Examples include "How might the *Roe vs. Wade* decision affect human rights issues?" "How can you apply what we have learned to . . . ?" A student, for instance, may know a rule of grammar and may even understand the rule. However, can she or he apply the rule to a new situation or context, for example, using it correctly in an essay?

4. Analysis—This higher cognitive domain of learning expects students to take a situation apart and to understand the relationship between parts. For example, you may show your third-grade class a picture of three groups of animals and ask them which group does not belong. The student is required to analyze the various characteristics to arrive at an answer. Key words here are *analyze, show, how, distinguish,* and so on. Examples include "Who can distinguish between fact and opinion in the article we just read?" "Why did the balloon inflate?" "How does the author use similes to convey an emotional impact to the reader?" "What is the difference between . . . and . . . ?"

5. Synthesis—At this higher level, students can creatively put elements or information together to form a new structure or idea. Key words here are *create, develop, devise, predict, invent,* and so on. Examples include "Given the elements of a lesson, you will develop an original lesson of your own, put together the carburetor, invent a machine that would make life easier," and so on.

6. Evaluation—This is the highest level, according to Bloom. Too often, teachers ask students to make judgments about something without challenging them with the prior levels of thinking or behavior. Evaluation requires students to state their opinions and justify their points of view or answers. Key words here are *decide, judge, discuss, choose, recommend, give your opinion, explain why, evaluate,* and so on. Examples include "Was the story good? Why or why not?" "Which technique would be better? Explain." "Who can tell the class what is wrong with . . . ?" This final level encourages critical reasoning and judgment.

[Mnemonic for recalling Bloom's Taxonomy: **K**eep **C**alm **A**t **A**ll **S**ports **E**vents]

Here's a little quiz for you. Identify the correct level of Bloom's Taxonomy in each of these objectives:

_____ 1. Given any art materials of your choice, you will create an oil painting using no more than four colors.

_____ 2. Given a number of objects that you have not previously seen, you will identify all those that are squares.

_____ 3. Given twenty new multiplication examples, you will solve 80% of them correctly.

_____ 4. Given eight poems written by European poets, you will determine the common theme.

_____ 5. From memory, list the nine planets in our solar system.

_____ 6. Given five master's theses, you will select the best research design.

Answers: 1. synthesis, 2. comprehension, 3. application, 4. analysis, 5. knowledge, 6. evaluation.

However, there is another problem in questioning that is frequently overlooked. The vast majority of questions asked in classrooms are by the teacher; students ask few questions, other than for assistance or clarification. If we are to develop active minds, not just passive and reactive ones, we must encourage students to learn how to formulate effective questions, for it is through questions that productive thinking occurs. Pupils must learn to question so that they can be critical processors and consumers of information. This process should begin in elementary school and not be delegated only to the higher grades, for learning and thinking patterns begin at early ages and shape all learning thereafter.

Here are several techniques to involve students in questioning (again, photocopy this information to share with teachers in need):

1. Classwork/Homework Questions—Have students make up questions for classwork or homework. For example, tell your students, "Make up five questions that would test whether someone had really understood the assigned readings. Make sure the answers are not in one sentence." This exercise promotes thinking, as well as learning how to write questions. As a bonus, you can choose a few of the best questions to duplicate and give to the class.

2. Journalist-Style Questioning—Invite a guest to class, but instead of having a presentation followed by "Are there any questions?" have students prepare questions in advance. Help students write questions that go beyond facts and lower cognition levels.

For example, students might prepare questions such as these for a visit by the school principal:

"Why did you select education for your career?" "What's the toughest part of your job as principal?" "Imagine you had the resources and influence to do anything you wanted in this school. What would you do and why?"

3. Questioning Through Games, Simulation, Role Playing—An excellent way for students to learn questioning is through games, simulation, and role playing. In each of these activities students are presented with a problem or situation in which they must ask questions to seek solutions.

For example, at a simple level, play games like "Changing Storybook History." Ask, "How could the gingerbread boy have outsmarted the fox?" "If you were Little Red Riding Hood, how would you have avoided the wolf?" For higher levels, simulations and role playing offer opportunity for mini investigations. For example, the teacher presents the following problem to her science class: "Over the past five years, there has been a dramatic increase in lung disease and asthma-like conditions in a particular city in the United States. Desiring to find the reasons for the increase and to correct the situation, city officials have called in a group of scientists to solve the problem. You are the scientists."

The team, or teams, might begin by posing questions that gain general information, such as where and what are the characteristics of the city, whether the problem has occurred elsewhere, and what are the symptoms of the ill residents. The students should lay a data foundation from which they can draw conclusions. Or the students might begin by listing possible reasons for the problem (pollution, a change in the people's diets) and then ask questions that gather data that might confirm or deny the hypotheses.

4. Student-Oriented Questions—When a student is having difficulty making a point or is confused, ask that student to formulate a question. This technique helps the learner to identify the area of concern and obtain the help she or he needs.

5. Waiting Time—What would your reaction be if someone started firing questions at you at the rate of two or three per minute? Such rapid

questioning appears to be typical of teachers around the country. After asking a question, a teacher waits one second or less for a student to answer. Then the teacher typically repeats, rephrases, or calls one second or less for a student to answer. Once the student has responded, the teacher typically waits less than one second before commenting on the answer or asking another question. We need to think about reducing the number of questions and getting more payoff per question.

In the pausing behavior of teachers, there are two important pause locations, called wait times. Wait time 1 is the pause following a teacher's question: whether students respond quickly or slowly, the teacher tries to wait. Wait time 2 is the pause after a student's response: the teacher tries to wait before commenting on the response or asking another question. When this second pause time is cut short, all the students' amplifying, qualifying, and speculation is chopped off by teacher intervention. Perhaps this is one reason that students in fast interactive systems speak in fragmented sentences. A child needs more time to verbalize.

Some poor types of questions:

1. Multiple—"What started the war with Iraq, and why did we get involved?"

2. Chorus—"Were we right?"

3. Leading—"Aren't the terrorists bad? Don't you agree?"

4. Addressed to the teacher—"Give *me* the answer." "Tell *me.*" (Use "us.")

5. Yes-No—"Did the girl go to the store?"

6. Calling a student's name before a question.

7. Not calling on nonvolunteers.

Procedure

1. List learning activities for the lesson.

2. Include pivotal (main) questions.

3. Include a brief sequential description of how the lesson will proceed.

See lesson plans later in the chapter for sample "procedures" or "lesson development."

Review

1. Reviews prior lesson or knowledge at outset

2. Stops to review after difficult material is presented

3. Provides a medial review (in middle of lesson)

4. Provides a summative review (at end of lesson)

5. Allows students to explain what they know

6. Teacher checks for understanding

In some lessons you might provide for a brief definite review that will help to clinch the concepts, skills, and understandings that have been taught in the previous lesson. Reviews may be conducted in various ways. You can pose a few thought-provoking and factual questions that ask for a summary of the previous lesson. You can pose a question that calls for a comparison or for an application. You can ask a student to present a summary of the previous lesson. After his presentation, the other members of the class should be asked to make corrections and additions.

Lesson in General

1. Well-paced

2. Worthwhile

3. Individualized

4. Varied student activities

5. Transitions smoothly

6. Medial and final summaries

7. Follow up

Tests

1. Appropriate to ability level

2. Clearly worded

3. Content valid

4. Clear directions

5. Sufficient time

6. Format varies

Homework

1. Grew out of lesson

2. Specific and well-defined

3. Varied—option driven

4. Differentiated—allow for different abilities

5. Explained and understood

Homework can be an important part of the student's process of learning. It can be an extension of a day's lesson, preparation for a new lesson, or the culminating activity for a unit of study. Homework assignments should be well thought out and relevant to the subject matter being taught. Here are some suggestions on this particular aspect of teaching:

1. Place the homework assignment on the chalkboard indicating the date it is due. Students can then copy down this information and refer to it when needed.

2. Give the homework assignment during class when there is adequate time for explanation and student questions.

3. Vary the type of assignment.

4. When possible use the previous day's homework as the basis for a class discussion, for review purposes, or as a lead-in for the new lesson you are presenting.

5. Homework assignments should be realistic. Do students have enough knowledge to do the work assigned? Will they have the materials needed at home to successfully complete the work? How long should it take to do the assignment?

6. Always collect the students' work the day it is due.

7. Grade the homework papers and return them to the students as soon as possible.

8. Notify parents if a student continually fails to do the assigned homework. Parents have a right to know if their son or daughter is not doing the assigned work.

Good schools have a clear and consistent homework policy, and teachers of different subjects in these schools coordinate homework assignments in terms of length and difficulty. Homework must be marked, reviewed, and graded. Know that research indicates that homework given and reviewed appropriately can raise student achievement (Walber, Paschal, & Weinstein, 1985).

Homework Guidelines

1. Develop classroom homework in line with school policy.

2. Coordinate amount and type of homework with other teachers.

3. Homework in early grades should not generally exceed 15 to 30 minutes, three times a week, and in upper grades 45 to 90 minutes four times a week. In high school, the time should be broken down by subject/class because no teacher has a clue as to the amount of homework given in other classes.

4. Homework must be relevant, interesting, and appropriate to the ability level of the student.

5. Never use homework as a punishment.

6. Don't use homework to introduce new ideas or concepts below high school.

7. Homework should sometimes incorporate nontraditional sources such as television, newspapers, the Internet, and so on.

8. Students should not be permitted to go home without fully understanding the homework (it's unfair to the students, and it irritates parents).

9. Don't give homework unless you will grade, return, and review it with students.

10. Differentiate assignments.

11. Keep parents informed of homework policy and their expected role.

12. Develop procedures for collecting homework and for checking homework.

Evaluation

It is always wise to evaluate a lesson plan. It is especially important if the lesson plan fell short of your expectations the first time around. Effective evaluation can be accomplished by considering the following questions:

- Were my aims relevant and realistic?
- Was I well prepared?
- Was my presentation organized and clear?
- Was my presentation varied enough?
- Did my students understand what they were doing and why they were doing it?
- Were my questions well phrased in language that the students could understand?
- Did the students respond properly to my questions?
- Did all the students listen to and take part in today's lesson?

Keep in mind these Strengths (S) and Weaknesses (W) of some aspects of your lesson. Again, feel free to use this information with new faculty.

MOTIVATION

S: based on need or interests sustained

W: no real motivation, overlong, not related to aim or lesson

AIM

S: definite, suitable, clear, achieved

W: lacking, not related to lesson, poorly worded, trivial

DEVELOPMENT or PROCEDURE

S: well-paced, sequential, varied approaches

W: digressions, confusing, poor transitions, inadequate content, too abstract, summaries poor

QUESTION and ANSWERS

S: clear wording, good distribution, pivotal questions, stimulate critical thought

W: confused wording, talking after question, no wait time, reliance on volunteers, poor distribution, one-word answers, repeating answers, "Tell me"

OUTCOMES

S: subject matter, skills, concepts, attitudes, lesson learned

W: not learned, no check for learning, skills not mastered, lack of remediation or enrichment

HOMEWORK

S: clear, appropriate, motivated, explained, individualized

W: missing, inappropriate, vague or confusing, too brief or too long

What's wrong or right with each scenario in Form 4.2? Complete the boxes.

Form 4.2   Lesson Evaluation Activity

	Good	Bad	Recommendations
1. Teacher to pupils who "chorus" out the answer: "Boys and girls, you should't call out that way. Charles, why shouldn't we call out our answers?"			
2. A teacher in an eighth-grade social studies class praises Committee A for having just completed an excellent report on the Hindu religion in India. She was especially pleased to note that each member of the committee read the report in a loud, clear voice.			
3. Teacher: "John, can you point out the Erie Canal on the map?" John goes to the map at the front of the board, but can't find the Erie Canal on the map. Teacher: "Can you help John, May?" May goes to the map and finds the Erie Canal. Teacher: "Class, is May right?"			
4. The reading teacher has organized four groups in her seventh-year corrective reading class. She starts instruction with the poorest group, as they need her help the most.			
5. In the industrial arts room, two boys are reading "Popular Machines" in the corner of the room while the other boys are at their respective stations working on projects.			
6. The drill in the mathematics class (seventh grade) consumes 10 minutes. All pupils work on the same examples and answer the questions successfully.			
7. The language arts teacher says to the class, "Before we start I'll tell you what to do. Read the story on page 8. Then answer the questions on pages 9 and 10. Write each word you don't know in your notebook. Now, get busy."			
8. In a reading lesson, the teacher notes that some pupils are reading aloud. She comments: "I hear someone reading aloud.			

	Good	Bad	Recommendations
How should we be reading?" Pupil: "To ourselves. Only with our eyes." Teacher: "Why shouldn't we be reading aloud?" Pupil: "It disturbs our neighbors." Teacher: "I'll read this paragraph. First I'll read it silently. (Ten seconds elapse.) Now I'll read it aloud. (She reads slowly.) Now which did I read more quickly?" Chorus: "The first time." Teacher: "Right. When you want to read to get information you read silently. In that way, you read faster. If you are reading to someone you would read aloud, but then you must read slowly or no one will understand you."			
9. The class is reading a passage silently. The teacher circulates around the room. Teacher: "If you need help, raise your hand. I'll come to you." No hands were raised. The class continued to work. Many pupils finished their work, took out other books, and read silently.			
10. In a social studies class: Teacher: "Howard, name the New England states." Student falters. Teacher: "George, let's see if you can do a better job than that."			

Some suggested sample answers (others may apply):

1. It's good to point out that choral responses do not allow teachers to assess who really understands the information. But don't first call on a student before or as you pose a question. Other students tend to tune out.

2. Effective use of positive reinforcement is a good thing.

3. Several problems here. Don't call on a student first and then ask a question. Other students will tune out. Avoid saying "Class, is May right?" Call on a particular student. Allow for wait time.

4. Nothing particularly wrong unless she always groups her class that way.

5. It depends on teacher's objectives. Is the teacher aware of what is occurring?

6. Does the teacher check for understanding? Do pupils always work on the same problem at the same time? Does the teacher differentiate her examples?

7. Busywork. What is the educational purpose of this activity?

8. Teacher models desired behavior and stimulates student thinking.

9. Teacher circulates and students seem to know class routines and procedures.

10. No attempt to assist the student, and the teacher denigrates the student.

Making Time for Instructional Leadership

"Providing instructional leadership? Who has the time?" asks an AP in an inner-city school in Los Angeles. "Certainly, we've learned about curriculum development and clinical supervision in graduate courses, but who has much time to really implement them when you're on the job," complains another AP in a suburban school in Westchester, New York. "Constant emergencies, student misbehavior, and being drained from lunch duties prevent me from working with teachers on the improvement of instruction," complains another AP. Anyone who has worked as an AP in a fairly large school setting realizes that it is difficult to devote much time to instructional improvement.

Overwhelmed and sometimes incapable of dealing with increased demands, APs think that devoting time to instructional improvement is impossible when, in fact, it is not only essential, but indeed possible. How then can an AP find the time to engage in instructional leadership? Here are some suggestions drawn, in part, from the work of Michael Fullan and Andy Hargreaves (1996): *Locate, Listen to, and Articulate Your Inner Voice.* To quote Fullan and Hargreaves (1996):

> Often, when we say we have no time for something, it's an evasion. What we mean is we have more immediate or convenient things to do with that time. Of course, bulletin boards and visual aids are impor-tant. But doing them doesn't make you feel personally uncomfortable. It isn't disquieting. It isn't a personal challenge. Listening to our inner voice is. It requires not just time, but courage and commitment too. (pp. 65–66)

Believe that you can make a difference. The importance of working to promote instructional improvement has been stressed. Commit to continuous improvement and perpetual learning as a foremost goal. APs must demonstrate the intestinal fortitude, if you will, to "push themselves to create the professional learning environments they want" (Fullan & Hargreaves, 1996, p. 82). More than that, APs must believe that they can make a difference (Denham & Michael, 1981).

APs who are comfortable with providing instructional support to teachers are likely to have been good teachers themselves. Moreover, they have the knowledge and skills to design and implement programs and activities that provide instructional growth opportunities for teachers. Such APs will find the time for instructional leadership because they value it and truly believe that it makes a difference in teacher development and student achievement. The mark of a good school is one in which instructional leadership is primary. Schools must consciously seek APs who are instructional leaders.

IN-BASKET SIMULATION

1. You are a newly assigned AP in a K–6 elementary school. The principal has indicated that she is not pleased with the results of the instructional program being provided to children who have been held over because of their lack of progress in class work and their poor performances on standardized reading and math tests. The holdovers are placed together in the same class on the grade. The principal requests that you review the situation and make recommendations to her. Describe with justifications four recommendations that you would submit to the principal for improving the instructional program for these held-over children so that they can function more effectively in the school. (Here are some suggested solutions: Develop a needs assessment committee to analyze past practices and suggest new directions; examine curricular materials used with students and consider more up-to-date curriculum materials; develop an instructional plan that stresses effective remediation; work out motivational strategies to excite holdovers; plan an action research study, e.g., pre/posttests, to determine effectiveness of program; etc.)

2. You are interviewing for an AP position, and the principal asks you the following questions: "What do you think about cooperative learning and peer tutoring? What do you see as their strengths and

(Continued)

(Continued)

weaknesses? When and how would you encourage teachers on the grades you supervise to use these strategies in their teaching?" Describe in detail your response. (Possible solutions here depend on your knowledge of cooperative learning and peer tutoring. Conduct a search on the Web to obtain additional information.)

3. Following you will find a transcript of an actual lesson. Read the transcript and follow these instructions: For each of the four (4) lesson elements listed below, indicate one (1) strength and two (2) weaknesses. Provide supporting evidence from the lesson for each strength and each weakness. Provide one appropriate recommendation for improvement for each cited weakness in each of the four (4) lesson elements. The recommendation must include an action to be taken to improve the weakness noted and it must be accompanied by an appropriate reason for its use. Begin your response to each lesson element on a new sheet of paper. Place the name of the lesson element at the top of each page. Be certain to number each page. Under each lesson element clearly identify each strength, weakness, evidence, and recommendation for improvement and reason for its use. (Answers will vary.)

LESSON ELEMENTS

1. Aim

2. Questioning

3. Assignment

4. Teacher

For example, let's say you are dealing with the "aim."

Strength	*Evidence*
1. Timely	1. 40th birthday of U.N. celebration

Weakness	*Evidence*
1. Aim not elicited	1. Teacher answered her own question with her stating of aim

Recommendation
Grade: 7
Ability: Average
Teacher: Mr. Jones
Lesson: Current Events

Mr. Jones, a well-respected seventh-grade teacher with 7 years of teaching experience, will be discussing violence in society for his weekly talk about current events.

Mr. Jones: "What can you tell me about violence in society?" (Calls on David, who has his hand raised.)

David: "It is a very serious subject."

Mr. Jones: "Yes, it is very serious, but what else can you tell me? What do you consider violent?" (Calls on Alisa, who has her hand raised.)

Alisa: "Hitting someone would be violent."

Mr. Jones: "That's right, Alisa. What else can you tell me?"

Alisa: "How about rape?"

Mr. Jones: "Right." (Calls on Billy Bob, who has his hand raised.)

Billy Bob: "I guess most crimes are violent."

Mr. Jones: "No, Billy Bob. Many crimes are not violent at all. What are some of the causes of violence?" (Calls on Freddie, who has his hand raised.)

Freddie: "Violence on TV shows and in the movies."

Mr. Jones: "Right, TV shows and movies that contain violence. Who else can tell me something that may cause violence?" (Calls on Skip, who has his hand raised.)

Mr. Jones: "Skip, what do you think?"

Skip: "Music."

Mr. Jones: "What do you mean, Skip?"

Skip: "Some music makes people violent."

(Continued)

(Continued)

Mr. Jones:	"I guess you're right." (Calls on Brian, who has his hand raised.)
Brian:	"Video games also contain violence."
Mr. Jones:	"Right, Brian, and that is a hot topic right now. A rating system on video games is in the process of being created."
Mr. Jones:	"What would you do, if you or someone you know was attacked?" (Calls on Jimmy, who has his hand up.)
Jimmy:	"I would get them."
Mr. Jones:	"What do you mean, Jimmy? You mean you would call the police and let them get them, right?"
Jimmy:	"No, I would do whatever they did to me and do it back, but worse."
Mr. Jones:	"That is why we have such a problem, because people want to get revenge instead of letting the police take care of things."
Jimmy:	"I don't care. I would do whatever it took to get them back."
Mr. Jones:	"Well Jimmy, that's wrong, and you would just get yourself in trouble. It would also be dangerous and somebody could get severely injured."
Jimmy:	"Laws that say you have to get in trouble for doing something back to someone are stupid, and I don't care if I hurt the person that did something to me."
Eddie:	(without being called on): "He's right. I would get the person back too. Why shouldn't I? And laws that do not let me, *are* stupid."
Mr. Jones:	"Guys, you have the wrong idea. The best course of action would be to call the police and let them 'get' the person for you."
Eddie:	(without being called on again): "No way, cops are idiots, and they would never get them. I would make sure I got them." (At this point the class is very noisy, and Skip is yelling at Jimmy.)
Skip:	"I still never got you back for breaking my CD player."

Jimmy: "Shut up, Skip. I told you it was an accident."

Skip: "Don't tell me to shut up, and it wasn't an accident." (Jimmy
                then punches Skip in the face.)

Mr. Jones separates the boys and sends them to the office. He instructs
Eddie to escort them so they do not fight on the way. Skip can be heard
yelling at Jimmy from down the hall.

Mr. Jones: "This is a perfect example of why there is so much violence
                today. People insist on getting even. This entire incident could
                have been avoided if Skip would have listened to Jimmy when
                he told him that it was an accident."

Eric: "But it wasn't an accident. I saw him break it."

Mr. Jones: "We better just end this discussion right now, before another
                fight breaks out."

Mr. Jones then assigns the homework.

The homework assignment is to write an essay on what steps can be
taken to protect people from violent crimes and make the neighborhood
safe.

5

Curriculum

There is no single right way to do curriculum . . . developing and implementing effective curricula are cooperative ventures in which district leaders, school administrators, and classroom teachers work together toward a common goal.

—Allan A. Glatthorn, *The Principal as Curriculum Leader*

———————◆———————

FOCUS QUESTIONS

1. How would you define "curriculum"?

2. What do assistant principals have to know about curricula?

3. Can APs serve as curriculum generalists, or do they also have to have subject expertise?

4. What do APs have to know about state and district standards?

5. How would you provide for curriculum leadership in your school?

Curriculum development is a dynamic, interactive, and complex process that serves as the foundation for good teaching practice. Assistant principals, as instructional leaders, must be actively involved in curriculum leadership. Parenthetically, it should be noted that although many APs are not involved in curriculum development, they should have some basic understanding. In addition, as the position evolves, greater attention to this area will likely occur. Such curriculum leadership is even more critical today because of national, state, and local attention to standards. APs and other educators are pressured to respond to the national movement toward standards-based education, including high-stakes testing, by raising standards and promoting uniformity of curricular offerings to raise student academic achievement. This chapter provides some suggestions for APs in implementing standards-based curricular reform. Respond to the items in the following survey, which serves as a guide to the rest of the chapter.

Form 5.1   Respond

Article I. RESPOND				
SA = Strongly Agree ("For the most part, yes") A = Agree ("Yes, but . . .") D = Disagree ("No, but . . .") SD = Strongly Disagree ("For the most part, no")	*SA*	*A*	*D*	*SD*
1. I see my role as AP to provide leadership in implementing state/district standards.				
2. I have a firm understanding of basic curriculum theory.				
3. I understand the connection between the purpose of education and curriculum development.				
4. I cannot help teachers in areas of curriculum because I am chiefly a manager who is good at administration, not curriculum.				
5. The knowledge base or content of a curriculum is more important than the needs of the learner.				
6. I am a progressive curriculum thinker and doer who believes in constructivist thought and practice.				
7. I know how to implement the Tyler Rationale.				
8. I can lead teachers in developing curriculum.				
9. I work with teachers on an ongoing basis to develop new ways to create meaningful curricula.				
10. I fully understand the history of standards-based reform initiatives in this country.				

The remainder of this chapter will address each of the statements mentioned previously.

Although APs must be able to provide leadership in terms of implementing state standards, they must also be able to engage teachers in curriculum development and revision. This chapter is divided into two main sections: (1) a general review of basic ideas and concepts in curriculum development and (2) a brief discussion of how to provide leadership when implementing mandated curricula.

Curriculum Overview

The study of curriculum development is very involved and important. In this curriculum overview, we will highlight a number of key elements to consider in curriculum design or revision. Some basic, yet essential information follows on the "purposes" of education that drive curriculum, on what we mean by "curriculum," and on types, sources, and approaches to curriculum development. Such information is critically important for APs working in this area.

Of Purpose

What is education? Why is obtaining one so important? What are the purposes of an education? Curriculum cannot be studied in isolation from these fundamental questions. Ask a few people, "Why do we need to be educated?" You might get some of these responses: to learn practical skills, for intellectual fulfillment, to make money, to appreciate democracy, to respect other cultures, and so on. An educated person seeks the following four notions that form four basic purposes of education:

1. Self-Realization—included in this broad category are ideas such as striving for intellectual growth, aesthetic interests, personal development, character building, self-worth, and so on.

2. Human Relationships—included in this broad category are ideas such as developing friendships, respecting others, fostering cooperation, developing ethical and moral reasoning, promoting democracy, and so on.

3. Economic Efficiency—included in this broad category are ideas such as work, career, money, to become an educated consumer, and so on.

4. Civic Responsibility—included in this broad category are ideas such as seeking social justice, tolerance for others, promoting world peace, respect for law and order, obligations to government, and so on.

Education is conceived as the deliberate, systematic, and sustained effort to transmit knowledge, skills, and values that a society deems worthy (Cremin, 1991). Schooling, Dewey reminded us, represents a small part of one's overall education. Life indeed educates. You may walk down the street one morning and meet a friend who "educates" you about a specific matter. Museums, TV, family, religious institutions, theater, libraries, salespeople, and prisons educate. Schools certainly play a vital role in education. Three purposes for education can be identified:

1. Helping children acquire knowledge and skills

2. Transmitting ideals and values of society

3. Preparing children to live creative, humane, and sensitive lives

These purposes of education and schooling are meant to stimulate your own ideas. Other educators may select different definitions and aspects to accentuate when speaking about education and schooling. The point, however, is that when we as educators attempt to translate these broad purposes into a program that offers intellectual and educational substance we enter the purview of curriculum. The curriculum field is devoted to the study and examination of the decisions that go into determining what gets taught. Hence, curriculum theorists deal with the following issues and concerns: epistemological (what knowledge is most worth), political (who controls this knowledge?), economic (how this knowledge is linked to power and goods and services), technical (how should this knowledge be made accessible to all students?), and ethical (is this knowledge morally sound?). As an AP you may address these theoretical concerns from an academic perspective, but when you work with teachers on a daily basis, you and they are most concerned with translating the broad or specific curriculum goals (standards) into practical lessons and units of instruction.

Of Definitions

Schubert (1993) notes that "the term curriculum is shrouded in definitional controversy" (p. 8). A discussion of this controversy, its history and implications, goes beyond the purposes of this chapter. Suffice it to say that curriculum has been variously defined. Some common definitions include (see Beach & Reinhartz, 2000)

- All planned and unplanned learning experiences in a school
- All that is planned and directed by teachers to achieve educational goals
- Planned and guided learning experiences and intended learning outcomes, formulated through the systematic reconstruction of knowledge

and experience, under the auspices of the school, for the learner's continuous and willful growth in personal-social competence

- Plans for guiding teaching and learning
- A work plan that includes both the content and the strategies for teaching and learning
- The careful planning, with the ultimate goal of increasing student achievement; not only the written plan or construct but the content, learning experiences, and results

What does *curriculum* mean to you? Many educators take curriculum for granted. It is sometimes and regrettably synonymous with the textbook. For many teachers and APs, curriculum is prescribed by district, city, or state agencies and presented as prepackaged mandates. Over the past several years, with great emphasis on high-stakes testing and standards-based education, educators at the school level have felt they have little control over what gets taught. APs can play an important leadership role here in conveying to teachers that mandated curricula do not necessarily stifle creativity and curriculum innovation.

Of Types

APs should help teachers distinguish among three types of curricula: taught, learned, and tested. Ideally, a logical and meaningful relationship exists among these three aspects of curriculum. Teachers in class every day involve students in meaningful lessons in various content areas. They teach students about ancient Greece, algebraic equations, geological formations, and poetry. Content may derive from prescribed curriculum guides or from an interplay of these guides and homegrown ideas. Although "taught," how do teachers ensure that curriculum is learned? Meeting the instructional needs of students by considering student involvement in curriculum or lesson planning may go a long way to ensuring that learning takes place. Teachers develop traditional and nontraditional means of assessment procedures to determine the extent to which students have learned.

APs play a key role in engaging teachers in discussion about curriculum. They can ask, "What is curriculum?" and "How can we take ownership of what is taught?" In doing so they encourage teachers to become stakeholders in curriculum development so that they can enrich the educational lives of their students through meaningfully relevant pedagogy.

A key ingredient to empower teachers to think about curriculum as an engaging instructional process is to help them explore their beliefs and values of education itself. APs can ask their teachers, "Where should our emphasis be placed when developing curriculum for our students: on knowledge itself, on the learner, or on what society deems most important?" The "Tripod View of

Figure 5.1   Tripod View of Curriculum

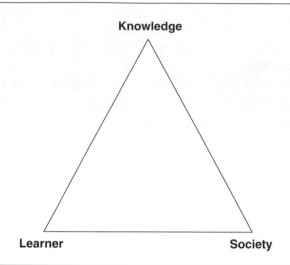

Curriculum" (Figure 5.1) is important to uncover fundamental beliefs of teachers and others in designing and developing curricula.

Of Emphases or Sources

Figure 5.1 depicts three emphases or sources in thinking about curriculum: subject matter (knowledge) considerations, learners' needs, or society's values. Which would you emphasize most? Is knowledge or subject matter most essential? In other words, should instruction be guided by subject matter considerations rather than by societal or learner needs? Should the needs of learners play the most prominent role in designing curriculum? What happens if the knowledge selected meets learner interests but does not meet societal expectations? Can you think of instances in which societal expectations drive curriculum?

Of Approaches

Three main philosophies or approaches to viewing curriculum relate to each of the three aforementioned curriculum emphases: essentialism, progressivism, and reconstructionism. The essentialist philosophy is based on the premise that curriculum is timeless as students pursue basic truths. Essentialists believe that the school's main purpose is to cultivate content mastery in order to stimulate intellectual development. The cultivation and accumulation of knowledge, for the sake of knowledge, is of great importance to an essentialist. What is most essential, put simply, is knowledge. Essentialist curricula stress the basic academic disciplines (liberal arts areas as well as science, mathematics, etc.).

Progressivism is a second approach to looking at curriculum. Promulgated by John Dewey (Cremin, 1964), progressivism emphasizes learning as an active process in which all students participate. Cooperative learning and problem-solving approaches are a high priority. Constructivism is aligned with progressive thinking. Constructivism is not a theory about teaching and learning per se; rather, it is a theory about the nature of knowledge itself. Knowledge is seen as temporary, developmental, socially constructed, culturally mediated, and nonobjective. Learning, then, becomes a self-regulated process wherein the individual resolves cognitive conflicts while engaged in concrete experiences, intellectual discourse, and critical reflection (Foote, Vermette, & Battaglia, 2001; Rodgers, 2002).

The principles of constructivist paradigms support the view of educators as informed decision makers. Accordingly, learning is a socially mediated process in which learners construct knowledge in developmentally appropriate ways and in which real learning requires that learners use new knowledge and apply what they have learned (Bransford, Brown, & Cocking, 1999; Vygotski, 1986). These beliefs emphasize "minds-on" learning. This endorses the belief that all learners must be intellectually engaged in the learning process by building on their previous knowledge and experiences and by applying their new learning in meaningful contexts. To become a constructivist (mediator of learning), the teacher preparation candidate must be guided by the development of the child, motivation, and learning. Thus central to expert instruction is a deep understanding of child development and a broad knowledge of the principles of pedagogy that serve as the blueprint for design of instruction that leads to student learning.

The third philosophy or approach to curriculum emphasizes the interests of society as most important in developing curriculum. Knowledge is important, according to this view, only to the extent to which societal goals are accomplished. Learners are expected to achieve content mastery over material deemed necessary by society. National and state standards are manifestations of societal expectations.

The "Tripod View of Curriculum," along with its curricular approaches (see Figure 5.2), are not necessarily either/or propositions. The three curricular emphases should come into play when undertaking any sort of curriculum development. Focusing on student needs and interests through a deep appreciation and understanding of child development comes into play in developing curriculum. At the same time, drawing learning experiences from broad-based discipline-centered curricula adds legitimacy and substance to any curriculum. Societal needs and interests must be considered in order to provide students with educational experiences and training that are useful so that students learn the fundamentals for various career choices.

Figure 5.2   Curricular Approaches

	Knowledge	Learner	Society
Essentialism	X		
Progressivism		X	
Reconstructionism			X

Of Models

In working with teachers to plan for teaching and learning, several curriculum models may serve as guides. One of the most helpful curriculum development models for teachers to easily implement is the one developed by Ralph Tyler (1949). His model is practical in the sense that APs can work with teachers to establish curriculum goals that can then be translated into instructional objectives. Through curriculum development, teachers identify learning activities to provide students with meaningful learning experiences.

Widely known as the Tyler Rationale, this useful model identifies four steps in curriculum development:

1. What educational purposes should the school seek to attain?

2. What educational experiences can be provided that are likely to attain these purposes?

3. How can these educational experiences be effectively organized?

4. How can we determine whether these purposes are being attained?

Tyler advocated detailed attention to these four questions in developing a curriculum. The basic idea to keep in mind about Tyler's model is that four steps are involved whenever you develop curriculum. First, state your objectives. According to Tyler, objectives must be stated in behavioral terms so that teachers can assess the extent of student learning. For example, state that the student will be able to identify four of five reasons why the Civil War started. Therefore, if the student can only identify two reasons, you know that student has not achieved the objective and needs additional work. Second, select learning activities. After objectives are articulated, select meaningfully relevant activities to help students accomplish the stated objectives. These learning activities should relate to the developmental stage of the student and should consider student needs and interests. Providing learning activities that motivate students is critical. Third, organize the learning activities. Learning activities should be concrete and sequential (i.e., one builds on the other). Learning experiences also must be well integrated, according to Tyler. That is, they should relate to each other so that students see some rhyme and reason to them and how they relate to the objectives. Fourth, develop a means of evaluation. You should develop performance measures to determine the extent of student learning. These may take the form of traditional testing (e.g., objectives tests) or alternate forms of assessment, although Tyler focused more on traditional means of evaluation. Additional information about Tyler's approach to curriculum may be obtained by conducting a quick Web search typing in "Tyler Rationale."

Three criticisms have been leveled at Tyler's model. First, learning that is merely identified with observed changes in behavior is limited in the sense that although some kinds of learning are likely to be manifested in observable behavior, many other kinds are not. Sometimes change may not occur immediately but may blossom months after a particular unit is taught. Long-term development of intellectual patterns of thought is not considered in the Tyler model.

A second problem arises when teachers precisely identify learning objectives in advance of instruction. Progressives such as Dewey, for instance, saw objectives as arising out of activity, giving that activity a richer, deeper meaning. Objectives, according to this criticism, do and should not always precede activity.

A third criticism of the Tyler Rationale arises from a simplistic view of evaluation or assessment. A unit of instruction, according to the Tyler model, is successful when measured outcomes match prespecified objectives. Sometimes the most important outcomes may not have been anticipated. Therefore, simply measuring outcomes aligned with prespecified objectives may miss significant student learning outcomes.

Notwithstanding these criticisms, APs can use the Tyler model, keeping in mind its limitations, to help teachers identify learning outcomes, develop learning strategies, and establish criteria for assessment. Note that alternate models exist. Consult, for instance, Pinar, Reynolds, Slattery, and Taubman's (1995) work.

Of the Curriculum Development Process

Three key curriculum development steps for teachers can be identified:

1. Planning for teaching and learning

2. Implementing the plan

3. Assessing teaching and learning

Figure 5.3 Operationalizing the Steps in Developing the Curriculum

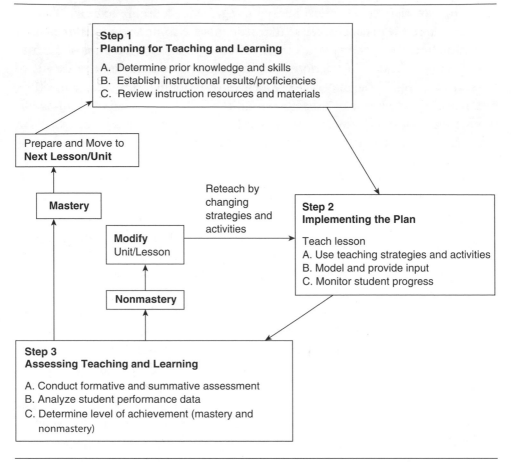

SOURCE: From Don M. Beach & Judy Reinhartz, *Supervisory Leadership: Focus on Instruction,* © 2000, published by Allyn and Bacon, Boston, MA. Copyright © 2000 by Pearson Education. Reprinted by permission of the publisher.

According to Beach and Reinhartz (2000), "These three steps provide a framework for supervisors to use in working with teachers in groups or individually as they develop a blueprint for teaching and learning in classrooms and schools" (p. 199). Figure 5.3 illustrates the three steps of the curriculum development process. The steps are cyclical, as the process begins and ends with planning. Units or lessons are modified and improved through this process.

Developing curriculum at the planning stage involves determining prior knowledge and skills of learners, establishing instructional outcomes, and reviewing appropriate resources and materials. As teachers and APs plan together at this stage, they reflect on the teaching and learning process. During a grade conference, for example, teachers and an AP can examine mandated curricula but still be free to develop and match instructional objectives with learner needs and abilities. Curricular modifications at this stage are possible and indeed recommended to plan for the most meaningful unit of instruction possible. Instructional practices, for instance, in an inclusive classroom will differ dramatically from a more homogeneous grouping of students. During this stage, teachers and an AP can review availability of appropriate resources and materials that support instruction. During this stage, teachers and APs address possible teaching strategies and activities, goals and objectives, assessment procedures (always keeping the end in mind), content or subject matter, and standards that must be met. APs play a key role in this opening step of the curriculum development process as they challenge and lead teachers to consider

- Content matched to the developmental level of students
- Prerequisite knowledge and skills before undertaking a new unit of instruction
- Inductive and deductive teaching approaches
- Selection and appropriateness of learning experiences
- Sequencing of learning experiences
- Selection and appropriateness of assessment instruments

Beach and Reinhartz (2000) remind us that "the success of the curriculum depends on the quality of planning and the decisions that teachers make as they prepare for instruction" (p. 201).

During the second step of the curriculum development process plans are implemented. Teaching is the process of implementing curricular plans. Curriculum and teaching are conceived as very much interrelated. During this step, teachers present their lessons using appropriate and varied strategies and activities. Teachers also model skills and monitor student progress (see Figure 5.3).

The third step of assessing teaching and learning is critically important. If students are not learning, the curriculum development process requires modifications. Perhaps instructional objectives need reconsideration, teaching strategies may need revision, or reteaching and review may be necessary. You, the AP, can assist teachers by engaging them in informal and formal conversations about units of instruction. You can assist teachers in gathering learning data from a variety of sources beyond the traditional pencil-and-paper test. Alternative forms of assessment are shared with teachers. These may include, among other things, student portfolios that include work samples and journal writing.

Of Quality

Glatthorn (2000, pp. 11–12) highlights several guidelines for developing quality curriculum, some of which are reviewed in the following discussion:

1. Structure the curriculum to allow for greater depth and less superficial coverage. Teachers should engage students in meaningful and detailed lessons that involve problem-solving projects and activities and critical thinking teaching strategies. Such activities and strategies form the basis for any topic to be covered during the course of the school year. Rather than rushing to "cover" topics or "teaching for the test," teachers should give students the problem-solving and critical thinking skills that they, on their own, can apply to any topic.

2. Structure and deliver the curriculum so that it facilitates the mastery of essential skills and knowledge of the subjects. Providing students a rich and deep knowledge base is primary but should be incorporated with problem-solving strategies that are realistic and meaningful to students.

3. Structure the curriculum so that it is closely coordinated. Coordinating content within lessons and among units over the course of the school year is imperative so that curriculum is sequential and well organized.

4. Emphasize both the academic and the practical. Relating content to the lived experiences of students is important to increase student learning. Hands-on activities, when feasible, are very much warranted.

REFLECT

As you read the information that follows, consider how constructivist theory influences your work in curriculum development.

How do people learn best? John Dewey (1899) said that people learn best "by doing." Hands-on instructional tasks encourage students to become actively involved in learning. Active learning is a pedagogically sound teaching method for any subject. Active learning increases students' interest in the material, makes the material covered more meaningful, and allows students to refine their understanding of the material.

Constructivist learning theory that supports active learning is essential in curriculum development. Constructivism is not a theory of teaching, but of knowledge and learning. Meaningful learning centers on the learner and is best constructed through collaboration and reflection around personal experience. Knowledge is meant to conform to the needs of the learner.

According to constructivist theory, people learn best when they are given opportunities to construct meanings on their own. How best to accomplish this lofty goal becomes paramount. Simply leaving students "on their own" is a wholly inefficient and ineffective way of stimulating reflective thinking. Teachers *must* guide students and provide thought-provoking questions or frameworks as they engage in these hands-on activities.

Again, how does constructivism influence your work in curriculum development?

_____

_____

_____

_____

Implementing Mandated Curricula

Increased interest in state and national standards has had a profound effect on curriculum development. APs should understand the historical context for this most current strand of standards-based reform initiatives. In doing so, they can ably assist teachers to work with mandated curricula but, at the same time, encourage them to view curriculum development as a viable, dynamic, and enriching process.

Raising standards and promoting uniformity of curricular offerings to raise academic achievement has been a long-established reform proposal (Seguel, 1966). Present efforts at establishing national or state standards should be viewed within a historic context. The first significant attempt to improve and "modernize" the American curriculum occurred in the 1890s. The Committee of Ten issued its report in 1892 under the leadership of Charles W. Eliot, the president of Harvard University. The Committee sought to establish new curriculum standards for high school students. Standards were established to enable all students to receive a high-quality academic curriculum (Kliebard, 1987).

Notwithstanding the lofty aims of this committee, it wasn't until the establishment of the Commission on the Reorganization of Secondary Education that the school curriculum actually changed. The commission issued its report in 1918 and advocated a diversified curriculum that made allowances for a variety of curriculum "tracks" for the varied abilities of students. Known as the "Cardinal Principles of Education," the findings of this commission endorsed a differentiated curriculum that emphasized, in part, the importance of vocational training for a large segment of students (Krug, 1964).

During the first half of the twentieth century, the College Entrance Examination Board (formed in the 1890s), the Scholastic Aptitude Test (the first SAT was administered in 1926), and the American College Testing Program (established in 1959) were the guardians of standards, as applied to the academic curriculum. As a result of the Russian launch of the first artificial satellite (Sputnik) in 1957, American education was attacked vociferously. Only months after the Sputnik launching, Congress passed the National Defense Education Act (NDEA), which poured millions of dollars into mathematics, sciences, and engineering. For several years following Sputnik, enrollments in high schools increased dramatically as did achievement scores in many academic areas. Academic standards, up until this time, continued to be driven by levels of student achievement and assessed by national standardized tests (Ravitch, 1995).

By the mid-1960s, however, the American school curriculum shifted from an academic orientation to a nonacademic one. Prompted by political and social reforms, educational reformers reconsidered their long-standing emphasis on academic curriculum standards. The easing of high school graduation and college entrance requirements were just two of many effects of educational reforms during this tumultuous era. Yet, by the late 1970s, criticism of nonacademic curricula focused on declining SAT scores and what was perceived as a general lowering of standards. With the election of Ronald Reagan in 1980, an era of unprecedented educational reform, focusing on a conservative political and educational agenda, was about to begin.

With the publication of *A Nation at Risk: The Imperative for Educational Reform*, a report by the National Commission on Excellence in Education (1983), attention was drawn to the assertion that schools had lowered their standards too much and that American students were not competitive with their international counterparts. The authors of this 1983 report were perturbed by the fact that American schoolchildren lagged behind students in other industrialized nations. The National Commission on Excellence in Education reported that, among students from various industrialized nations, U.S. students scored lowest on seven of nineteen academic tests and failed to score first or second on any test. The Educational Testing Service (1992) reported similar results. Moreover, the study found that nearly 40% of U.S. seventeen-year-olds couldn't perform higher-order thinking skills.

Pressure to improve the quality of American education by articulating concrete standards for performance increased. Consequently, a spate of national and state reports continued throughout the 1980s, each advocating fundamental educational change. Commitment to democratic ideals and the influence of public education was reinforced once again in 1986 with the publication of the report, sponsored by the Carnegie Foundation, titled *A Nation Prepared: Teachers for the Twenty-first Century* (Carnegie Forum on Education and the Economy, 1986) and the Holmes (1986) report. The national curriculum reform movement was catapulted into prominence and action with the Education Summit held in 1989 by then President George Bush and state governors. A year later, in his State of the Union Address, President Bush affirmed his commitment to excellence in education by establishing six national education goals to be achieved by the year 2000. Signed into law by Congress during the Clinton administration on March 31, 1994, "Goals 2000" proclaimed, in part, that by the year 2000 "U.S. students will be first in the world in science and mathematics achievement" and "Every school will be free of drugs and violence and will offer a disciplined environment conducive to learning."

The adoption of national goals has been a major impetus for the increased attention to standards at the state level. In 1991, the U.S. Congress established the National Council on Educational Standards and Testing (NCEST), which encouraged educators and politicians to translate somewhat vague national goals into content curriculum standards. NCEST recommended that educators establish specific standards in specific subject areas. The National Council of Teachers of Mathematics (NCTM) led the way by publishing standards that quickly influenced textbook companies and testing agencies. These national curriculum reforms inevitably affected state educational reforms. More than forty states have revised their curricula to reflect the standards they established.

Continuing in the tradition of standards-based education, President George W. Bush signed into law the "No Child Left Behind Act of 2001," a reauthorization of the Elementary and Secondary Education Act Legislation of 1965. The purpose of the new legislation was to redefine the federal role in K–12 education and to help raise student achievement, especially for disadvantaged and minority students. Four basic principles were evident: stronger accountability for results, increased flexibility and local control, expanded options for parents, and an emphasis on teaching methods that presumably have been proven to work.

What can this brief history of standards-based education teach us about the current interest in revising curriculum and raising standards? First, standards-based education is with us, and our success is due in large part to ensuring that we address these standards. Merely accepting state or national standards with grim resignation does not do much to lift our spirits about teaching and learning. APs can provide strong leadership by helping teachers see standards as useful guides and opportunities to expand learning experiences. Ensuring that students are receiving instruction that meets national or state standards will increase confidence in teachers that they are preparing students in the best manner to meet expectations of a global economy. With the exploding knowledge and information age and the rapid changes in technology, a growing demand for internationally competitive workers indicates to teachers the import of their work. APs need to stress to teachers that as professionals they must meet demands placed on them by state and national agencies, while at the same time indicating "advantages and disadvantages of externally imposed standards" (Glatthorn, 2000, p. 5). Such honest and open discourse will empower teachers to develop effective strategies to best use and implement standards. Although content areas to be taught are specified in standards-based education, APs should remind teachers that creativity is still essential to ensure that the very best instructional practices take place. Following the three steps of curriculum development, explained in the previous section of this chapter (see Figure 5.3), goes a long way to keeping curriculum alive and engaging for both teachers and students.

IN-BASKET SIMULATION

1. You are an AP responsible for coordinating and overseeing the elementary school's (K–5) art program. As the new AP you learn that art has been a neglected part of the curriculum because of the emphasis on preparing for the citywide reading and math tests. Teachers are complaining that they have little time for teaching the arts. Describe the steps you would take to develop, vitalize, and incorporate the art curriculum in Grades 3 and 4. (Answers may vary; use information in this chapter.)

2. You are an AP at a local high school that has an excellent reputation for its rigorous curriculum. You receive an anonymous note in your mailbox informing you that Mr. O'Hare is teaching topics not part of the prescribed history curriculum and that students will not be prepared for the statewide competency exam. Assuming that the allegations are verified, describe your actions. (Here are some possible solutions or approaches: Observe the teacher; speak with the teacher in private to ascertain reasons; explain why adherence to curriculum is important while supporting teacher's creativity to extend the curriculum, where and when appropriate; with teacher's permission, bring issue of "teaching to the curriculum" up at a faculty or grade conference for open discussion; etc.)

3. You are assigned as an AP in a middle school in an urban area in which teachers complain that they are unable to teach their subject area because of the students' poor reading skills. Outline the steps you would take in dealing with the teachers and in improving the reading abilities of the students. Include the techniques, services, and personnel you would utilize. Discuss the curriculum development initiatives you would take.

(Base your curriculum response on information in this chapter but feel free to vary your responses in terms of your knowledge of dealing with reading difficulties—be sure to include discussing the problem with an expert in the field.)

4. A teacher complains that he's "tired of teaching to the standards." He tells you, "I'm losing my creativity. I have no time to teach what I think is important." How would you respond to this teacher? (Here are some possible approaches: Open up lines of communication by affirming the teacher's comments; offer to discuss the matter in private; discuss strategies of how the teacher could include his teaching creativity and still address standards; etc.)

6

Program Development and Evaluation

Successful program development cannot occur without evaluation. Program evaluation is the process of systematically determining the quality of a school program and how the program can be improved.

— James R. Sanders, *Evaluating School Programs: An Educator's Guide*

◆

FOCUS QUESTIONS

1. Can you think of a situation in which an AP would have to develop a new school program?

2. What is the first step you would take to initiate a new program in your school?

3. Why is program evaluation an important skill for an assistant principal?

4. What are some major questions to consider in developing an evaluation plan?

5. Have you ever undertaken a formal evaluation of a program? If so, what caveats would you recommend to a novice AP?

As an AP, you'll most likely want to implement some sort of instructional program and then establish procedures for evaluation. I recall my first position as an AP in an elementary school in New York City when I was confronted with some serious misbehavior in the upper grades by a few students at risk. I decided to initiate a unique program to deal with this troublesome situation (Glanz, 1995). In establishing this martial arts program I also realized that its effectiveness had to be assessed. This chapter uses that martial arts program as an example of how you as an AP might evaluate a program. The realistic case is specific but the guidelines are generic. Respond to the items in the following survey to set the tone for the chapter.

Form 6.1   Respond

Article I. RESPOND				
SA = Strongly Agree ("For the most part, yes") A = Agree ("Yes, but . . .") D = Disagree ("No, but . . .") SD = Strongly Disagree ("For the most part, no")	SA	A	D	SD
1. I fully understand how to conduct evaluation research.				
2. I possess the skills to conduct evaluation research on my own.				
3. I have undertaken an extensive review of a program in my school within the last year.				
4. The first step in program evaluation is to establish goals and objectives.				
5. I believe that data must be collected from a variety of sources in any program evaluation.				
6. Many of my colleagues rarely, if ever, undertake serious program evaluation.				
7. I can conduct a program evaluation on my own without assistance from others.				
8. Program development and evaluation are essential skills of good APs.				

What Is Evaluation Research?

Evaluation research is the gathering of data in order to make a decision. Assistant principals need to make many decisions on a daily basis. Unfortunately, many of these decisions are made hurriedly and without the scrutiny of thoughtful, scientific investigation. What seems to be most expedient at the time is often the most important criterion for determining, for example, the fate of a new music program. Based on my experiences in schools, I have found that when assistant principals are trained in sound research methodology, decisions are made more intelligently and equitably. To determine the fate of the new music program, the AP would collect appropriate data from a number of sources before making the final decision to disband, modify, or even continue the music program. The value of evaluation research is its ability to help the AP make informed educational decisions.

What to Evaluate?

Evaluation research can be divided into three types (the 3 P's):

1. Program evaluation

2. Procedural evaluation

3. Product evaluation

APs are usually involved in making judgments about the effectiveness or desirability of various programs. They can and should assess school goals and priorities, academic programs, extracurricular activities, school policies and rules, school climate, and special projects, among other things.

An AP might ask questions such as these: "Does the new program work?" "What impact does inclusion have on the attitudes of teachers?" or "Does the whole language program affect reading achievement levels among third graders?" Program evaluation that is regular, dynamic, and ongoing contributes greatly to the overall effectiveness of the school organization.

A very common form of decision making is known as procedural evaluation. Evaluation of this nature is concerned with examining school procedures such as safety plans, scheduling, emergencies, supply distributions, and so on. APs can assist the principal in this process. I am in favor, however, of APs getting more involved in instructional improvement (see Chapter 4) and not in procedural evaluation, which can be delegated to other school personnel.

APs also need to evaluate facilities and equipment, financial plans, school resources, and instructional materials on an ongoing basis. Product evaluation deserves special analysis; that is, however, beyond the scope of this chapter.

Establishing a Program

The following eight steps will guide you in establishing almost any program in a school:

Step 1: Needs Assessment

APs and other leaders sometimes attempt to change or implement programs without considering many important factors. The first task of a competent AP who wants to start any sort of program is to analyze the situation by describing and identifying problems or areas of concern. In other words, an AP should undertake a needs assessment.

How should a needs assessment be undertaken?

1. Reflect by posing questions

   - Does the school need a gifted program?
   - What evidence indicates that the school might need such a program?
   - Has a gifted program ever been implemented before?
   - If so, what happened to the program, and why was it discontinued?
   - What will my new program contribute to addressing the needs of gifted students?
   - Who is considered a gifted student?
   - How do I (we) plan to implement such a program?

Posing key questions is the first step in implementing any program. You should address these questions in collaboration with other supervisory staff and interested faculty.

2. Observe

Prior to making any decision about implementing the program, "walk around" the school getting to know the faculty, staff, students, and parents. Observe students and teachers at work. Get a sense of the culture of the school. We call this MBWA. You know what that is, right? *Management By Wandering Around.* This doesn't mean aimless wandering but rather purposeful observation. Too many APs and principals, from my experience, manage their schools from the main office, rarely observing and talking with their faculty and staff on a daily basis. Successful implementation of your program involves "getting out there" and finding answers to some key questions:

   - What are faculty interested in?
   - Who are the influential members of the faculty?
   - What instructional strategies do teachers commonly employ?

- Do students seem enthusiastic about learning?
- Are parents involved in the instructional/curricular program?
- Is there some grassroots support for the need of change?
- Who might you confide in and ask to participate in the initial stages of program implementation?
- What resistances to change exist?

Observing includes examining records, school files, and profiles. Examining records such as cumulative student folders, school profile sheets that provide summaries of standardized test scores, and teacher files may give you some valuable clues as to the direction you may take to implement this program. Such an analysis will help ascertain existing strengths and weaknesses that should be addressed during the initial stages of program implementation.

3. Meet with key personnel

Meeting with key school personnel, informally (through MBWA) and through formal invitation, not only will demonstrate your concern about faculty input into program development but will provide valuable insights that observation alone cannot offer. Meet with the following personnel, among others: teachers, principal, union representatives, parents (especially PTA president and board), superintendent, coordinators, guidance counselors, secretarial staff, lunchroom personnel, deans, and other supervisors. Speak with everyone! Why? For four reasons:

- To allow them to voice their concerns and opinions about the new program
- To apprise them of possible future developments
- To share information with them
- To invite their input in terms of suggestions, comments, and participation

Although such attempts at shared leadership may be unusual and difficult to attain, my experiences have convinced me that effective and lasting change occurs best through collaboration among faculty, staff, administrators, community, and students.

4. Establish a needs assessment committee

A final step in needs assessment might be to form a committee comprised of interested teachers, supervisors, parents, and students to assist in the implementation of the program. This committee can plan implementation of the project and engender support from other faculty and interested parties.

Step 2: Goals

The second step you should take once you've decided that the program is needed is to develop short- and long-term goals. Framing a vision of what this new program has to offer is critical in program development. Goal development should be done collaboratively by involving as many stakeholders as possible. Setting up a committee for this purpose is recommended. This committee can be comprised of the same members as the needs assessment committee, although involving others is advisable. This committee would be charged with

- Brainstorming goals or program objectives
- Prioritizing goals
- Disseminating goals to faculty, staff, and community

Whenever you form a committee to evaluate something, keep in mind these three questions:

- Why have we formed a committee? (purpose)
- What are our short-term plans? (objectives)
- What are our long-term plans? (goals)

Short-term goals should be accomplished within a one- to six-month framework. Examples of short-term goals are establishing criteria for admission into the gifted program; forming a planning committee of two teachers, one staff developer, one parent, and a student; and so on.

Examples of long-term goals are increasing parental involvement by 10%; decreasing teacher burnout; implementing a portfolio program next year for the upper elementary grades; raising standardized reading test scores by 15%; and so on.

Step 3: Administrative Aspects

Administrative or logistical concerns should be worked on throughout the implementation phase. As an AP, you should attend to the following concerns, among others (in collaboration, of course, with the principal):

- Staffing considerations
- Scheduling
- Advertising
- Room allocations
- Ordering materials and supplies
- Securing funding sources

- Publicity
- Delegating responsibilities

Step 4: Supervision

Supervision is a process that involves strategies to enhance instructional improvement (see Chapter 3). An AP is concerned with facilitating an environment conducive to learning.

A competent AP should attend to *PCOWBIRDS*. For a complete discussion of this concept see Chapter 4.

P = Plans

C = Conferences

O = Observations

W = Workshops

B = Bulletins

I = Intervisitations

R = Resources

D = Demonstration Lessons

S = Staff Development

Step 5: Curriculum

Curriculum includes all the planned experiences, programs, and subjects that are designed to enhance student learning. As an AP, you are always actively engaged in curricular and instructional matters (see Chapters 4 and 5). Too much time is often spent on what I call "administrivia." Administrative exigencies must, of course, be attended to, but instructional improvement will not be enhanced without direct and specific attention to curricular concerns. Suggestions include

- Reviewing current curriculum guidelines and other instructional materials
- Reviewing materials for instruction (e.g., texts, workbooks, computers, etc.), making certain that curriculum materials are matched to appropriate instructional levels of students
- Arranging assembly programs, fairs, exhibits, contests, and other incentives such as banners, T-shirts, buttons, and so on

- Facilitating an interdisciplinary curriculum
- Encouraging curriculum development and renewal (Glatthorn, 1994)

Step 6: Parents and Pupils

Implementing any program involves parental input in terms of advisement and participation. While once being interviewed for an assistant principalship, I was asked if I believed in parental involvement. Not wanting to offer the usual or typical canned response, I rose from my seat and demonstrated for the committee my commitment to parental involvement in the following way:

"Let me show you what I mean when I say that parental involvement is essential." I held up a blank piece of paper (Illustration 6.1). I continued, "Within a school there are basically three groups of individuals. There are faculty (including administration and teachers), there are students, and there are parents." As I mentioned each group, I drew a small oval until I developed the configuration seen in Illustration 6.2. "Quite often," I lamented, "when faculty work on their side, and the parents work on their side, all without partnership and commitment, the students are left in the middle." As I mentioned "the faculty," I placed a dot in the center of the left-hand oval; as I mentioned "the parents," I placed a dot in the center of the right-hand oval, and as I mentioned "the students," I merely pointed to the center oval. I ended up with the configuration in Illustration 6.3.

"When this happens," I continued, "when there is no communication and teamwork between these two sides, the whole system can get looking pretty unhappy." As I said "when there is no communication," I drew the curved line above the three ovals. Then, as I said, "the whole system can get," I drew the curved line under the three ovals. The configuration now resembled the sad face shown in Illustration 6.4.

"But let's add teamwork. Let's get everyone working together to help our children. When parents and faculty work together constructively, the whole school is unified." As I mentioned "working together," I drew a large, encompassing oval around the sad face so that it looked like Illustration 6.5.

"Then," I concluded, "thanks to teamwork and the spirit of cooperativeness, students will succeed and we will have a happy and functioning school; one we may all be justly proud of." As I said the last words, I turned the drawing around 180 degrees. Before the eyes of the committee, it turned into the happy face seen in Illustration 6.6.

Illustration 6.1

Illustration 6.2

Illustration 6.3

Illustration 6.4

Illustration 6.5

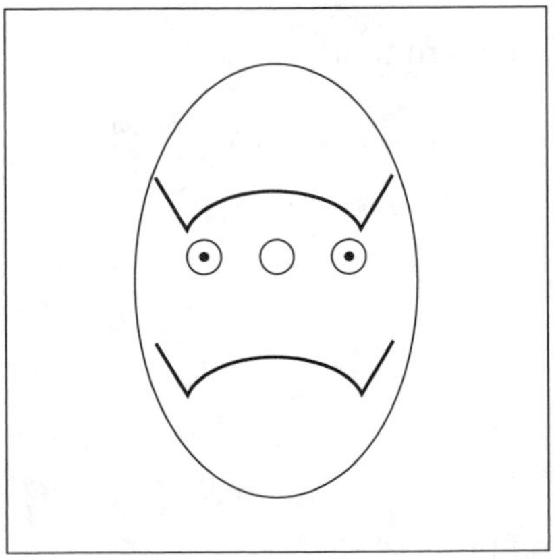

Illustration 6.6

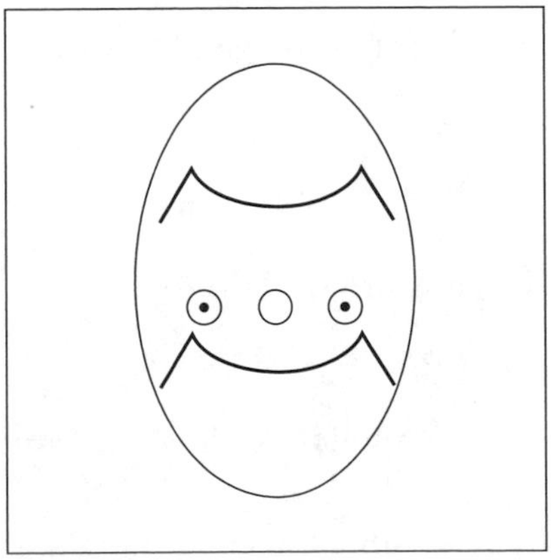

SOURCE: From Susan Mamchak & Steven Mamchak, *School Administrator's Public Speaking Portfolio*, 1983. Reprinted with permission of the Center for Applied Research in Education/Prentice-Hall.

Although this was a somewhat contrived and simple demonstration of my philosophical commitment to parental involvement, several committee members did smile, and I'm certain I effectively communicated my point. Involve parents in any reasonable way possible. Here are some suggestions:

- Invite their participation on needs assessment and goal committees through formal and informal invitations.
- Sponsor an open house at which you will provide refreshments and outline the nature of participation you desire.
- Develop a "parent hotline" so that parents may keep abreast of what's happening in the school.
- Invite parents to "parent-student" picture night.

Step 7: Resource People

Program implementation involves the active participation of several other personnel, depending, of course, on the nature of the program. The following individuals may be valuable resources: principals, guidance counselors, teachers with special expertise, social workers and psychologists, specialty coordinators from the district office or neighboring townships, lunchroom and office staff, health department officials, consultants, and so on.

Step 8: Evaluation

As defined earlier, evaluation is a decision-making process. In an era of accountability in which productivity is demanded, evaluation assumes greater priority and attention. How can we as APs increase productivity?

1. Set goals

2. Determine where we are

3. Identify strategies for getting where we want to be

In a nutshell, when we evaluate, we want to answer two fundamental questions:

1. How are we doing?

2. How can we improve?

Keep in mind the following points:

- Evaluation is a comprehensive, ongoing process.
- Evaluation is formative and summative. Assessing progress along the way is imperative. Why wait six months or a year before realizing that

changes are warranted? Formative evaluation allows for program adjustments and modifications. Research has indicated that programs that incorporate formative evaluative measures are more likely to succeed. Summative evaluation leads to one of three conclusions:

1. Modification of program or procedure

2. Elimination of program or procedure

3. Continuation of program or procedure

- What should be assessed or evaluated? Any programs, practices, and procedures should be evaluated—such as, among others, school goals and objectives, parent-teacher conferences, assessment procedures (including report cards), faculty meetings, assembly programs, music programs, administrative procedures, drop-out rates, attendance policies, schoolwide discipline plans, curriculum materials, pupil achievement, accounting procedures, school climate, and so on.

How to evaluate? Keep this mnemonic in mind: *ROTC*.

R = records and rating scales—examine records, develop rating or attitudinal surveys, and checklists

O = observations—both formal and informal

T = tests—standardized and/or nonstandardized

C = conferences—with everyone

A General Evaluation Plan

In developing a general evaluation plan, keep in mind these points:

1. What is the purpose of evaluation?

2. What needs to be evaluated?

3. What are your goals?

4. How will data be collected?

5. How will data be organized and analyzed?

6. How will the data be reported?

Problems are inevitable in program evaluation. Keep in mind these five steps for solving problems:

1. Analyze the situation

2. Examine research (data collected or evidence)

3. Examine results

4. Develop alternative solutions

5. Act (modify, discard, or continue)

A Mnemonic for Establishing a Program

I highlighted and detailed eight (8) steps to consider in implementing any educational program. Can you recall the eight steps? Here are two acrostics:

1.
Negative
Grades
Always
Scar
Children's
Parents
Really
Emotionally

2.
Never
Give

A

Strange
Child
Permission to
Run the
Exam

PROGRAM EVALUATION IN FIVE STEPS

The following steps of program evaluation were employed when I evaluated a program that I had established in a school while serving as AP. The discussion that follows is based on information gleaned from Sanders (2000).

The program I evaluated was first established at a public elementary school to address some of the needs of at-risk students. What made this program noteworthy was that martial arts training was incorporated as part of an overall curricular approach aimed at assisting selected fourth and fifth graders who were either currently involved in gangs or likely to join them. Program evaluation involved the following five steps:

I. Focusing the Evaluation Is Composed of Three Steps

1. Clarify evaluation purposes

2. Clarify what is to be evaluated

3. Identify questions to be answered

The purpose of our evaluation of the martial arts program was twofold:

1. To monitor pupil progress academically and socially. The intent was to conduct formative (in-progress) evaluations of the students' academic and social progress.

2. To monitor pupil motivation. The intent was to provide insights about the effort and persistence among student participants.

Our primary purpose for evaluating the program was to determine whether or not a program of this nature, which had never been attempted in our school before, should be continued and expanded to include other students at risk. Formative evaluative steps would enable us to monitor the program on an ongoing basis. Midcourse corrections could be made if necessary to improve the quality of the program. A summative evaluation was planned at the end of the school year by accumulating overall data relating to our two purposes outlined earlier as well as bringing in an outside consultant to provide his reactions to the program. The consultant was a principal of a school in another district who was also a black-belt instructor in the martial arts.

After clarifying evaluation purposes, another set of decisions was needed to get a clear sense of what was to be specifically evaluated. Specific criteria were identified separately for each of the evaluation purposes noted previously. Five specific aspects were identified for pupil academic and social progress:

1. Incidence of aggressive behavior (physical fights with other students and/or physical acts toward faculty and staff)

2. Degree to which basic school and class rules were adhered to

3. Rates for tardiness and attendance

4. Number of homework assignments completed

5. Number of in-class assignments completed

Two specific aspects were identified for pupil motivation:

1. Degree to which students demonstrated effort and persistence in class

2. Degree to which students demonstrated effort and persistence in martial arts class

Once we had a sense of what was to be evaluated, evaluation questions were posed:

A. What were the expected academic outcomes for students who participated in the martial arts program?

B. What were the expected social outcomes for students who participated in the martial arts program?

C. Were students motivated to participate in in-class and school-related functions as well as in the martial arts class itself?

D. How well were the students performing on the expected outcomes noted previously?

E. To what extent was the program meeting expectations of principal, assistant principal, martial arts instructor, teachers, parents, and student participants?

II. Collecting Data

In order to answer each of the evaluation questions, sources of information and evaluation methods for each evaluation question had to be identified. Scheduling the collection of data and assigning responsibility for collecting data was also attended to.

Sources of data collection were culled from existing resources such as school files and records, direct observation of the program, and people in any way connected to the program. Evaluation methods that were deemed appropriate and feasible were matched to each evaluation question as follows:

A. What were the expected academic outcomes for students who participated in the martial arts program?

Data collection methods: teacher and pupil interviews, teacher-made tests, and checklists for completed assignments

    B. What were the expected social outcomes for students who participated in the martial arts program?

Data collection methods: teacher, supervisor, and pupil interviews, number of reported suspensions, number of times students were reported to AP's office for misbehavior, attendance reports, and observations

    C. Were students motivated to participate in in-class and school-related functions as well as in the martial arts class itself?

Data collection methods: teacher, supervisor, and pupil interviews, attendance reports, observations, student journals and portfolios, and visual anthropology or film ethnography (Marshall & Rossman, 1999)

    D. How well were the students performing on the expected outcomes noted earlier?

Data collection methods: methods noted previously through formative and summative evaluations

    E. To what extent was the program meeting expectations of principal, assistant principal, martial arts instructor, teachers, parents, and student participants?

Data collection methods: interviews and questionnaires

III. Organizing and Analyzing the Data

Evaluation methods provided much qualitative information. Much data was especially gathered through the use of multiple observers, multiple data collection methods, and extensive descriptions. Field notes, thick descriptions, transcripts of interviews, written responses to questionnaires, student journal entries, and copies of written documents, files, and reports were organized and analyzed according to each evaluation question. My concern was to summarize the data collected as accurately and clearly as possible. At every opportunity, I attempted to verify and validate the findings by getting reactions from people involved in the project.

IV. Reporting the Data

Results of this program evaluation revealed that the students at risk who participated in this integrated school/curricular martial arts program improved in the following ways:

Academically—Although teachers initially reported little, if any, change in the numbers of completed homework and in-class assignments, by the end of the sixth month of the program teachers did in fact state that these assignments were increasingly being completed. Teachers who were interviewed stated that they were pleased by this academic progress. Teachers attributed this success not necessarily to the martial arts program per se, but to the close contact with and supervision of these students by supervisors and the martial arts instructor. In fact, the martial arts program did provide an incentive for these students to improve academically.

Socially—Teachers and supervisors reported fewer incidences of aggressive behavior exhibited by these students. A reduction in the number of discipline referrals was clearly evident. Classroom teachers also reported greater adherence to rules and procedures, as did teachers on lunch duty. Improved attendance and tardiness rates were noted.

Motivation—Classroom teachers and the martial arts instructor related that these students demonstrated greater effort, interest, and enthusiasm.

Expectations—Results from interviews, questionnaires, and informal observations and talks with parents, teachers, supervisors, and students themselves revealed positive feelings about the curricular/martial arts program. Teachers and parents, in particular, asserted that they expected students to continue to improve.

Throughout the course of the evaluation, adult participants were informed about the evaluation process and the progress being made toward its completion. Time was spent obtaining comments from teachers, supervisors, and an outside consultant regarding any possible errors or omissions of evidence and other plausible interpretations that were missing. It was decided that the publication of an article in the district newsletter describing our program could enhance efforts to expand the martial arts program to possibly include a larger sample and even expand the program to other schools. Reports of this evaluation, then, were to be disseminated throughout the district.

V. Administering the Evaluation

Administering this evaluation plan was a complex and arduous undertaking. Many logistics had to be considered, including scheduling data collection, allocating time for data analysis, and budgeting. Although budget constraints were minimal, scheduling problems emerged fairly regularly. At times, certain teachers, due to their own pressures and concerns, did not readily provide needed data. Programs had to be occasionally adjusted and arrangements coordinated with participants. Establishing and maintaining open communications among all participants was a priority. Anonymity of participants was ensured.

In sum, in order to assess the effectiveness of our martial arts program, I attended to five basic tasks in program evaluation (Sanders, 2000; also see Wholey, Hatry, & Newcomer, 1994): focusing the evaluation, collecting data, organizing and analyzing the data, reporting data, and administering the evaluation.

CHAPTER SUMMARY

Can you name the eight steps to establishing a program?

_____

_____

_____

_____

_____

Hint: NGASCPRE

What about the five steps in planning an evaluation?

_____

_____

_____

_____

_____

Hint: FCORA

REFLECT

Can you think of a situation in which you can easily apply the eight steps to program development and the five steps to program evaluation?

_____

_____

_____

_____

IN-BASKET SIMULATION

1. The principal of the elementary school to which you have been newly appointed as the AP has been notified by the superintendent that each school must establish its own gifted education program. The principal assigns you to establish and evaluate the program's effectiveness and to provide a full implementation plan within three months. Describe the steps you would take to establish and evaluate the program. Be sure to include goals and objectives, staffing considerations, criteria for selection, curriculum issues that need to be addressed, materials and resources needed, and so on. Be as specific as you can. (Answers may vary but be sure to include steps provided in this chapter.)

7

Why Didn't They Teach Me This Stuff in Graduate School?

Short years ago, the assistant-to-principal was closely associated with clerical chores, with emphasis on such items as checking roll books, stamps, and textbooks. Sometimes, he was assigned solely to be a disciplinarian.

—Gilburt, "On Being an Assistant Principal"

FOCUS QUESTIONS

1. What have you learned in graduate school that adequately prepared you for the assistant principalship?

2. Why don't you think APs have time for curriculum development and instructional leadership?

3. Why are many APs relegated to serving as chief disciplinarians in schools?

4. How would you respond to those who say that assistant principals require little formal training in graduate school because all they need to know they can learn on the job?

5. Describe the realities of the assistant principalship to someone who asks, "What do APs do anyway?"

New APs are simply not prepared to assume the roles and responsibilities they are given because their graduate school training deals little, if at all, with matters of how to handle discipline and administrative duties such as lunch duty. This chapter, therefore, will principally deal with two areas of responsibility that were probably not addressed in your graduate education for the assistant principalship: how to deal with discipline matters and how to coordinate lunch duty. APs deal with, of course, many other noninstructional or curricular matters, many of which are learned on the job. This chapter will also provide some concrete suggestions for the following items which, according to my colleagues, were rarely addressed in school yet deserve treatment: developing a master schedule, the AP's role in special education, strategies for running effective meetings, and methods for involving parents. Respond to the survey that follows to guide you through this chapter.

Form 7.1   Respond

Article I. RESPOND				
SA = Strongly Agree ("For the most part, yes") A = Agree ("Yes, but . . .") D = Disagree ("No, but . . .") SD = Strongly Disagree ("For the most part, no")	SA	A	D	SD
1. I was adequately prepared in graduate school to face the realities of my role as AP.				
2. I am an effective disciplinarian.				
3. I can coordinate a schoolwide discipline plan.				
4. I see my role as AP to help teachers better manage their classroom.				
5. I feel comfortable in my classroom management knowledge base to conduct workshops for teachers in my school on developing a personalized discipline system.				
6. I believe that classroom discipline plans must be well coordinated with schoolwide discipline plans.				
7. I was fully prepared to coordinate lunch duty before I became an AP.				
8. I should be responsible for overseeing the school safety plan.				
9. APs essentially learn the job on the job.				
10. I am willing to participate in all noninstructional duties in my school.				

Dealing With Discipline

Teaching is a challenging, complex art and science that demands not only knowledge and skill but empathy, caring, and commitment. Frequently frustrating and exhausting, good teaching encourages, inspires, and arouses that latent spark within each student. Still, teachers are confronted with difficult, seemingly insurmountable obstacles that can be puzzling and exasperating. Student misbehavior, for instance, may drive a teacher to the very limits of his or her endurance.

The principles and practices of effective discipline and classroom management are among the most important professional concerns that practicing educators confront daily. The public's attitude toward education, assessed by Gallup Polls sponsored by Phi Delta Kappa, indicate that discipline is one of the most intractable problems public schools must contend with. Further, teachers maintain that student misbehavior is perhaps the most troublesome and disconcerting problem they face in the classroom. The resultant frustrations associated with student misbehavior not only increase levels of fatigue and stress but negatively impact teacher performance.

Compounding the difficulties associated with classroom management and discipline is the fact that teachers are often ill-prepared to deal with inappropriate student behavior. Ineffective suggestions such as "not to smile until Christmas" or that a well-planned lesson will always eliminate disruptive student behavior are out of step with current realities that confront classroom teachers.

Unfortunately, there aren't ready-made prescriptions to manage student behavior, nor are there specific techniques that apply to all classroom situations. Despite the assertions of some who attempt to promote their particular "discipline system," no "one best system" of classroom management exists. An effective disciplinarian utilizes an array of sound strategies to meet specific problems in particular situations in the classroom.

Therefore my purpose in this section of the chapter will be to assist you, as an AP, in helping teachers develop their own system of discipline based on their unique needs and circumstances.

Let's define some terms and review some key information (ideas culled from Charles, 2001):

Behavior—all the physical and mental acts people perform. For example, a hiccup, neither good nor bad, is a human behavior.

Misbehavior—the label given to any behavior that is considered inappropriate in a given context or situation. That hiccup, for instance, when performed intentionally in the midst of a reading lesson may be considered misbehavior.

Five Levels of Misbehavior—(in declining level of severity)

1. Aggression—the most severe form of misbehavior, including physical or verbal attacks by students

2. Immorality—acts such as cheating, lying, and stealing

3. Defiance of authority—when students refuse to comply with regulations

4. Class disruptions—perhaps the most common form of misbehavior: acts including calling out, getting out of seat without permission, and general fooling around

5. Goofing off—included in this category are those students who, for example, don't participate, daydream, and don't complete assignments

Discipline—steps taken to cause students to behave acceptably

Classroom Management—the process by which discipline strategies are implemented

Rules—guidelines that inform students how to act in class (e.g., please walk in class)

Procedures—deal with a specific activity and how to do it (e.g., how you expect students to line up for lunch)

Three Stages of Discipline

1. Preventive discipline—refers to those steps a teacher may take to preclude misbehavior from occurring in the first place

2. Supportive discipline—refers to those steps a teacher may take to encourage student behavior during the first signs of misbehavior

3. Corrective discipline—refers to those steps a teacher may take to restore order once misbehavior occurs

Six Elements to Consider About Classrooms

1. Multidimensionality—many events and acts occurring (i.e., the classroom is complex, not a simple environment)

2. Simultaneity—many things happening at the same time (i.e., teachers must remain cognizant and think quickly)

3. Immediacy—rapid pace at which events occur (i.e., events occur at an unbelievably fast pace)

4. Unpredictability—difficult to always know for sure what may occur (i.e., you are dealing with human beings, not inert raw materials, and therefore it's difficult to predict behavior)

5. Publicness—teach on stage (i.e., teachers are role models and must always remain aware of the effect they have on their students)

6. History—class develops a culture of experience and norms that provide the basis for future interactions (i.e., each class is different and assumes a "personality" of its own)

DEVELOPING A PERSONAL SYSTEM OF DISCIPLINE

A plethora of effective strategies and techniques for maintaining classroom management are available to assist teachers in positively redirecting student behavior. Rather than developing a list of "do's and don'ts" that have ephemeral benefits, to say the least, and more importantly don't address their specific needs for maintaining classroom management, this part of the chapter can assist teachers in developing their own system of discipline. Suggestions for APs in working with teachers on managing disciplinary concerns are included.

Student misbehavior, at some level, is inevitable. However, effective classroom managers are proactive, not reactive. They take effective steps to minimize occurrences of misbehavior. Preventive measures indicate a teacher's awareness that misbehavior might occur and establish guidelines for appropriate classroom behavior.

Still, misbehavior will occur in the best of classrooms. That's why supportive measures are necessary to quell disturbances at the outset. Corrective guidelines are necessary when preventive and supportive steps are inadequately implemented or ineffective with more severely disruptive students.

Developing a discipline system or plan that incorporates each of these three stages of discipline is essential to effective classroom management. Let's discuss some of the basic components of each stage and practical recommendations for their implementation.

Preventive Discipline—This is really the planning stage. It includes all the steps teachers take to establish a positive classroom environment conducive to student learning. Their effectiveness as a classroom manager depends on their ability to thoughtfully develop a plan that anticipates misbehavior and establishes guidelines for appropriate behavior. You as AP can play a critical role in helping them develop this plan by conducting workshops for them, meeting with them to codevelop plans, and providing the supervisory support to ensure successful implementation.

1. Develop a stimulating and worthwhile lesson. Although a well-planned lesson alone is not an assurance that misbehavior will never occur, it's certainly advantageous in motivating and encouraging student participation. Incorporate a wide array of teaching strategies such as discussion groups, oral

reports, role playing, cooperative learning, and peer tutoring. Intentionally deliver instruction in a variety of ways to meet the diverse learning-style needs of your students. Here are some effective teaching strategies matched to each of three learning style preferences:

    a. Visual preference— For those who learn best by seeing, use pictures, films, charts, flash cards, computers, and transparencies.

    b. Auditory preference—For those who learn best through verbal instructions, use lectures, oral directions, records, peer tutoring, mnemonic devices, and song.

    c. Kinesthetic preference—For those who learn best by doing, use manipulatives, 3-D material, debate, projects, pantomime, interactive videos, physical movement, and plays.

2.   Organize the physical environment. The teacher seating plan can affect student interaction. Regardless of the physical setup (e.g., rows, groups, horseshoe, pairs, etc.), make sure all seats are positioned to ensure visibility and allow teachers to gain proximity to any student as quickly as possible. Ensure that the room is uncluttered and that learning centers, sinks, clothing areas, and entrance are accessible. Although I personally like a nicely decorated room, too many classrooms are overly decorated, and some students may be easily distracted. An AP can serve as "another set of eyes" to offer suggestions to teachers.

3.   Develop five rules and procedures for appropriate behavior. Rules establish clear expectations for student behavior. Rules let the students know what performance and behaviors teachers deem acceptable. APs play a vital role in terms of ensuring that classroom rules are in sync with schoolwide rules. For instance, if schoolwide bathroom policies mandate that girls are to go to the bathroom in pairs, then the classroom rules for bathroom should reflect such a policy. When teachers disagree with a schoolwide policy, discussion with an AP is critical.

Teachers should develop five rules for acceptable classroom behavior that they'll review the very first day of class and reinforce throughout the year. Teachers can have their students add a rule or two that they feel should be included. Guidelines for rules follow:

    a. State rules in a positive way (e.g., "please walk in the classroom," not "don't run"

    b. State rules clearly (e.g., "listen in class" is too ambiguous—"look at the person who is speaking to you" is clearer and conveys the behavior expected

    c. Make sure certain rules are consistent with school rules

Plan on common procedures to be reviewed with the class (e.g., lineup procedures, what to do if students miss an assignment, and procedures for walking into the classroom after lunch).

Research indicates that effective managers spend time teaching rules and procedures. Don't worry that instructional time will be initially lost. Teaching and reinforcing rules and procedures are times well spent and may do much toward preventing inappropriate behavior.

4.   Use positive reinforcement or "catch 'em being good." Everyone wants encouragement and recognition. Effective teachers use varied and frequent reinforcement for acceptable behavior. As often as possible they should use some of these reinforcers:

   a. Social reinforcers—Use verbal acknowledgments such as "I appreciate your hard work," "Keep it up," "Wow, I'm impressed," and "Excellent." As a classroom teacher for many years I always kept a list of 100 different expressions I could use. After a while, my students couldn't wait to hear which one they would receive! Also, use nonverbal reinforcers such as a smile, pat on the back, a handshake, and so on. Reinforce every student at least once a day.

   b. Graphic reinforcers—Use marks, checks, stars, happy faces, and so on.

   c. Activities—Acknowledge students who comply with rules and regulations. Don't wait until they misbehave for them to receive your attention. Allow the student to assume monitorial duties, sit near a friend, have free time, read a special book, have extra time at the learning center, care for the class pet, and so on.

   d. Tangible reinforcers—Use a token reward system in which students can earn coupons, for instance, to obtain prizes. They can earn points to receive a special positive phone call from the teacher to the parents!

5.   Who's the boss? Teachers are the authority in the classroom. They must develop high standards for performance and expectations for behavior. They must be fair and consistent when implementing the discipline plan. When administering discipline, the teacher should always try to do so in private. Above all else, the teacher should attempt to build rapport with students. Although adherence to classroom and school policies is necessary, the manner in which the teacher interacts with students is critical. Keeping a sense of humor is especially important. Although the teacher is the "boss," an effective teacher will never be "bossy." Rather, the teacher should involve students in decision making and self-monitoring of behavior.

Supportive Discipline—Any experienced teacher realizes that the best plan can't deter all misbehavior from occurring. Misbehavior is inevitable. Notice what happens in this scenario:

[John throws a crumpled paper from his seat into the garbage pail. Teacher doesn't respond. A moment later Mary throws a paper. Teacher doesn't react. Then Steve throws a paper.]

Teacher: Stop that, Steve.

When a teacher ignores a breach of a class rule, others are likely to follow suit. In this case, when the teacher finally did reprimand a student, it was too late. Steve's complaint may be "Why didn't you yell at John or Mary?" This may escalate into a verbal argument between teacher and student. In addition, Mary and John may be upset with Steve for implicating them.

When teachers notice a student breaking a class rule they shouldn't ignore the behavior, but should rather "nip it in the bud" by employing one of many types of supportive discipline techniques. The teacher's personal discipline system should include numerous supportive strategies. If the teacher is new, I suggest he or she keep these techniques written on small index cards for easy reference. These are some of the techniques that can be used to support discipline:

Withitness—Jacob Kounin (1977) maintained that teachers who were aware of what was happening in their classrooms were less likely to have problems escalate. For instance, they're working at the board with one student and notice John throwing paper from his seat. Teacher says, "John, that's your first warning." You're "withit." You've communicated to the entire class that you're aware of what's happening and have put John on notice. Being "withit" will nip problems in the bud when they first occur.

Send signals—When teachers see Jose misbehaving, they should communicate dissatisfaction with a nonverbal signal such as a frown, stare, or wave of the hand.

Use physical proximity—When teachers either anticipate a problem or see one initially developing, they should walk over to the student as nonchalantly as possible and stand near her.

Corrective Discipline—Despite best efforts to prevent student misbehavior and support discipline, there will be times when more stern or corrective measures are necessary. Teachers should be encouraged not to hesitate to use these corrective measures. They communicate that teachers care and are willing to insist on proper classroom behavior.

According to Charles (2001), "Your corrective techniques should be neither intimidating nor harshly punitive, but instead only what is necessary to stop the misbehavior and redirect it positively." Teachers should consider the following corrective techniques:

Be assertive. Lee Canter's (1989) model has gained popularity among some educators because it trains teachers to act more assertively. Canter's distinction among three different response styles is instructive:

    a. Nonassertive style—"For the fifth time, won't you please stop throwing that paper?"

    b. Hostile style—"If you throw that paper one more time I'll kick you out of here, stupid!"

    c. Assertive style—"I want you to stop throwing that paper and get back to solving those problems."

Assertive responses are effective corrective measures because they make teachers' expectations known clearly and in a businesslike manner. Assertive teachers are ready to back up their response with action.

Invoke consequences for misbehavior. When teachers reviewed their class rules, students should have been apprised of the possible consequences for noncompliance. Therefore, when Ernest refuses to stop throwing paper, a teacher might say, "Ernest, you're refusing to work so you'll have to complete your assignment during recess." In developing their own system, teachers should note the nature and severity of each consequence tied to a specific type of misbehavior. These guidelines should be publicized and reviewed periodically.

Contracting. I have personally found this corrective measure very effective. APs should remind teachers not to confront a student, if possible, in the midst of acting out in class. If the student must be removed (e.g., time out), then they should do so. Trying to meet with the student as soon after an incident as possible to develop a cooperative contract for appropriate behavior is recommended. This should involve an actual written document (usually effective in elementary or middle schools) in which an agreement between teacher and student is reached regarding rewards for good behavior and consequences for inappropriate behavior. Effective contracts should:

    a. Be mutually agreed upon, not teacher imposed

    b. Be realistic and short-term

    c. Be specific (e.g., "work on math problems for 30 minutes a day over the next week" is better than "study hard")

    d. Specify how long the contract will be in effect

    e. Specify rewards

    f. Be signed by student, teacher, principal, and parent

Time out. This is a disciplinary strategy in which a student is removed from a situation and physically placed in a designated time-out area. Time out is particularly effective when the student's misbehavior is precipitated by peer pressure. Although effective for younger children, time-out areas located outside your classroom are more effective with older students (teachers should plan time-out areas with your involvement). Teachers should keep in mind these four steps when implementing time out:

    a. Designate a time-out area that is isolated to sight and sound as much as possible. The area should be undecorated and as uninteresting as possible.

    b. Student must remain idle without work or amusement to occupy the time.

    c. Establish a specific time (e.g., five minutes). I used to place a stopwatch at the desk so that the student could self-monitor.

    d. Follow up. When the student returns to his or her seat, make sure the teacher says a few words about expectations about future behavior. If a teacher must briefly meet with the student after class, then he or she should do so.

SEVEN STEPS TO DEVELOPING A PERSONALIZED DISCIPLINE SYSTEM

Successful teachers develop a discipline plan unique to their interests and needs. As AP, you should encourage your teachers to develop their own system of discipline. Review the following information with your teachers:

1. What are their needs? The first step in developing a discipline system is to prioritize the needs for classroom management. They should make a list of those conditions essential for their ideal classroom (e.g., students should have assigned seats, work quietly, respect fellow classmates and teacher, hand in work on time, etc.)

2. What are their rules and procedures? They should develop a list of acceptable behaviors, culled from their needs list, that they want to teach and reinforce.

3. What are the consequences for compliance and noncompliance? They should compose a list of positive and negative consequences tied to each rule and procedure.

4. What strategies will they employ? They should list specific strategies they feel comfortable implementing in each of the three stages of discipline: preventive, supportive, and corrective.

5. How will they implement their plan? They should plan to teach their system through discussions, role playing, and practice sessions. They should review and reinforce their plan throughout the year.

6. How will they test their plan? They should start putting their system into action. They should be fair and consistent, yet flexible. They should modify their plan as needed.

7. If problems arise, as they most certainly will, should they give up? Never! All students can learn self-control. All students want acceptance and recognition. The system teachers establish can satisfy student needs for social acceptance. Teachers should always seek to expand the repertoire of strategies in their plan. They should seek assistance and guidance from others. If they believe all children can learn, then they believe that all children can become sincere, courteous, responsible, and disciplined.

CONCLUSION

Do experienced teachers need a plan? Regardless of experience, all teachers need to plan strategies for dealing with nonconformity to classroom rules and procedures. Their personalized plan should be reviewed periodically and matched to the unique needs of their current class. As AP you have a special role to play in assisting teachers with their personalized discipline plan. You also serve as an invaluable means of support in terms of reinforcing their discipline plans. Students can easily sense when the plans of the supervisor conflict with the teacher's plan, or vice versa.

As the AP, it is vitally important that you establish, publicize, and reinforce a schoolwide discipline plan that is matched closely with the teacher's plan. As mentioned earlier, the rules of both systems (school and classroom) must be coordinated to support one another. Here are a few suggestions for reinforcing your schoolwide discipline plan:

- Conduct frequent workshops for teachers on classroom management and discipline.
- Review school expectations for behavior and challenge teachers to include them in their classroom plans.
- Support teachers for adhering to their plans (e.g., if a student is legitimately sent to your office, make sure you support the teacher's actions by reprimanding the student and take appropriate action rather than making the student a monitor).
- Monitor student compliance to classroom and schoolwide rules and procedures (e.g., conduct assemblies).
- When conducting an investigation of a discipline infraction make sure you gather all facts before arriving at a decision.
- Ensure that every teacher has developed and implemented a sound discipline plan.

REFLECT

Below you will find a personalized system of discipline developed by a teacher. Discuss how you would or could use this plan with your teachers.

My Personal System of Discipline by Rachel Schwab

I teach a first grade boys' mainstream class. My curriculum includes reading, writing, math, social studies, and science.

My students are usually not used to the rules and behaviors that are expected in a first grade classroom. Rules, procedures, and reinforcers (especially negative ones) are a new experience for them.

Therefore I must be careful to present and explain my rules, positive consequences, and negative consequences in a clear, easy-to-understand, and precise manner.

Personal Belief Statement

One of my main goals as a teacher is *to make a difference in the life of a child.* I aim to accomplish this, first, by getting to know each child well, as the whole person that they are. I also aim to create a positive and warm atmosphere in my classroom, in which every child is encouraged to reach his full potential, knowing that I believe in him. I do my best to maintain a fun and interesting atmosphere, as well, so that my students' early experience in learning will be one of fun and enjoyment. To this end, I show my students love and respect, yet at the same time set specific limits so that my students' self-esteem grows while they learn responsible behavior.

These smaller goals are meant to culminate in my belief in making a difference in the life of a child, by helping their year in first grade be one of accomplishment and growth in a pleasant atmosphere. In this way, their first experience in "real" school is a positive one.

My Needs

One of my most basic needs is a well-managed classroom: where students know what is expected of them, where the room is orderly, and where routines are set with room for flexibility when necessary.

Another personal need is for each child to feel that he gets what he needs, academically and emotionally, so that he can grow in knowledge, self-esteem, and responsibility.

It bothers me when my students are mean to each other or laugh at one another; therefore I do not allow these behaviors in my classroom. This includes teaching my students to act respectfully toward one another and to show caring behavior for each other, both of which are important social skills.

Within the set routines, it is important for there to be a lively, warm and positive atmosphere in my classroom, so that my students can develop a lifelong love of learning.

My Rules

1. Follow directions.

2. Raise your hand before you speak.

3. Work quietly in your seat without disturbing others.

4. Be kind and polite to each other.

5. Speak with respect.

I selected these rules because they focus on two of my major concerns: maintaining order in the classroom and promoting a positive classroom atmosphere with warmth and respect. If these conditions are not met, the potential for learning cannot be fulfilled.

The first rule is important during independent work, group work, and during transition times to promote good classroom management.

The second and third rules help maintain a calm, pleasant environment in a classroom. Of course there must be some flexibility within these rules, such as during discussions and specific activities.

The third, fourth, and fifth rules are particularly helpful in maintaining an atmosphere of caring and respect, that is, a positive environment. Caring, trust, and respect must be present between students as well as between the teacher and her students.

Rule 4 also encourages good social skills, which are important skills in a first grade classroom.

I have separate rules for when the students work in cooperative groups. Because the nature of the setup is so different, my expectations for when students work together differ from when they are working independently or when I am teaching them.

(Continued)

(Continued)

Cooperative Group Rules

1. Take turns talking quietly.

2. Listen to each other's ideas.

3. Praise each other's ideas.

4. Help each other when asked.

5. Stay together until everyone is finished.

6. Talk about how you worked well together and how you can improve.

So as not to overwhelm my students with so many rules, I do not present all the rules to my class the first week of school. Cooperative group rules are first presented and modeled when we begin working in groups.

Before posting the rules, I read them to my students, and we discuss them and why they are so important in a classroom setting. We also role-play them to make sure that the students understand them.

I find that having rules for the various ways that we learn helps create an orderly classroom and a pleasant learning environment. Children like to know procedures and what is expected of them. The time spent teaching rules is always regained when a classroom can be managed well because of the rules and procedures that are in place.

Positive Consequences

1. Catch them being good—use verbal praise.

Not only do children themselves respond to the praise they are given, it causes a positive ripple effect. The other students also want to be recognized, so they imitate the behavior that was praised.

2. Students who behave well can get a positive note, a "happy gram" sent home at the end of the day. I also make positive phone calls home, and I find that parents are thrilled to receive them.

3. My students love helping me, or being chosen to be my monitor. Students who follow the rules and behave are chosen to be monitor for various tasks.

4. Children earn the right to be first in line for library or recess by behaving appropriately.

5. For extra-special recognition, I have a child take a note to the principal, detailing his good behavior.

6. Depending on the class and the time of year, I have some type of reinforcement system set up, either individual or row charts, or classwide contests. In these ways, the children can accumulate a predetermined number of stickers to reach a larger reward. The rewards vary from tangible prizes to extra recess, planned trips, or mini-parties.

I also have small rewards that I give out randomly. In this way, the children get the incentives they need without constantly "working for a prize."

Negative Consequences (in increasing order of severity)

1. Eye contact—The student knows that I am aware of what he is doing, yet he has a chance to correct his behavior before it becomes an issue.

2. Warning—The child receives a verbal warning about the inappropriate behavior.

3. The child works away from the group for 5 minutes.

I do not increase the amount of time spent working away from the group. I usually find that due to their age, it either works the first time or the child continues to act up, and a longer period of time only serves as a greater distraction to others.

4. Lose 2 minutes of recess.

I do not take recess away completely, because children need that time to move around and be part of social interaction. I do find that losing 2 minutes of recess is very effective and still allows them some time to take part in recess activities.

5. Call parents.

6. Go to the principal.

Severe clause: Go to the principal.

(Continued)

(Continued)

My rules, positive consequences, and negative consequences are sent home to the parents as our classroom discipline plan. The parents discuss it with their children, sign it, and return it to me. This way, they know how I run my classroom and can better understand anything that might happen.

Preventive Discipline

1. My students and I discuss the rules at the beginning of the year. We review the rules and the necessity for them during the year. The class understands what is expected of them.

2. I plan the use of my classroom space to maximize visibility and proximity and use these techniques.

3. "Withitness"—When students realize that you know what's going on, and that you won't put up with it, they don't try to test you as much. Also, if you exude self-confidence and an air of authority, students respond appropriately.

4. When my lessons are well planned, organized, interesting, and creative, students are less likely to misbehave because they are interested and actively participate.

5. Rewards from my list of Positive Consequences—They reinforce positive behavior and serve as an incentive for others as well.

Supportive Discipline

1. Establish eye contact with the student.

2. Use of nonverbal signals—shaking head, hand signals, and so on

3. Proximity control/touch

4. Verbal warning

5. Discussion of relevant rules and firm demand for appropriate behavior (includes broken record technique)

6. Use of rewards from my list of Positive Consequences.

Corrective Discipline

1. Firm demand for specific behavior.

2. Implement negative consequences (listed earlier), based on the severity of the behavior.

Closing Statement

This plan will be the foundation of my personal system of discipline. The system gives me a way of addressing my classroom needs. It corresponds with my philosophy toward children and teaching. However, classes differ from year to year, so I need to be aware that not all methods will work every year. I also believe that it is important to remain flexible because students vary greatly from one another and because each child is an individual with specific needs. This is not in conflict with remaining consistent. Consistency is one of the most important details of any system of discipline. Students can understand what is expected of them and know the inherent consequences both positive and negative. However, there will always be students with special needs who demand greater understanding. Because of this, a certain amount of flexibility for rules and consequences must be anticipated. Sometimes students need individual behavior plans, charts, or systems. I have found that students understand and respect this concept, as long as they feel their needs are being addressed and they get what they need. They can accept that fair is not always equal, because everyone has individual needs.

I feel that being aware of my needs in the classroom, as well as of my beliefs in dealing with children, can help me become a reflective practitioner, a teacher who thinks about what I am doing in the classroom and what I hope to accomplish. This, together with knowledge and ideas of positive consequences and negative consequences, and an understanding of my students, will hopefully assist me in reaching my goal of making a difference in the life of a child.

Discuss how you would or could use this plan with your teachers.

_____

_____

_____

_____

_____

REFLECT

In Table 7.1 you will find a rubric for assessing classroom management. Discuss how you would or could use this rubric with your teachers. **Assess how effective a classroom manager you are.**

_____

_____

_____

_____

_____

_____

Table 7.1 RUBRIC for Assessing Classroom Management

RUBRIC for Assessing Classroom Management

Name of teacher:

Date:

Observer:

Comments:

Performance Dimension	Unsatisfactory	Emerging	Proficient	Distinguished
Monitoring Seat Work	Teacher works extensively with one group while ignoring others; Unaware of off-task students; Fails to reinforce those on-task; Employs ineffective supportive disciplinary techniques to off-task students; Unaware of what students are doing; Does not monitor students effectively	Teacher scans room occasionally; Somewhat aware of what students are doing; Misses some off-task behavior; Stays near their desk or concentrates attention to one half of room; Aware when arguments occur and separates students; Tries to implement monitoring strategies, albeit inconsistently	Teacher aware of what is occurring in classroom; Uses effective verbal and nonverbal communicative techniques to monitor student behavior; Gives praise most of the time and reprimands those students who are not following class rules; Spends a bit too much time with each child; Help provided as needed; Uses eye contact and scans the room every few minutes; Attentive to monitoring seat work	Teacher very well aware of what is occurring in the classroom; Appears to have "eyes in back of head"; Able to do several tasks simultaneously; Defines rules of what's expected from students during seat work; Offers social praise to those who are working; Able to immediately "nip in the bud" a child who may seem off-task; Able to "overlap" and do two things at the same time; Spends just the right amount of time with each child; Monitors seat work very well

(Continued)

159

Table 7.1 (Continued)

Performance Dimension	Unsatisfactory	Emerging	Proficient	Distinguished
Transitions	No well-defined set of procedures for transitions; Students unsure how to proceed; Remains in fixed position rather than circulates; Long delays before start of activities; Teacher unprepared for next activity and takes time putting belongings away or taking out material for next subject; Teacher has little idea of the importance of transition	Teacher may give instructions during transition; Instructions vague; Verbal praise may be given to students complying with the routine; Teacher may put transitional times on the board; Delays between activities are no more than five minutes; Teacher prepares materials, but spends too much time setting up; Teacher aware of the importance of transition but has difficulty in facilitation	Teacher has a set schedule posted in a prominent place in classroom; Students aware of when to expect changes; Students can respond to instructions efficiently most of the time; Procedures for transitions are reviewed weekly and practiced so that when actual transitions occur there is little loss of instructional time; Students are reinforced for good transitions; Teacher models desired behaviors to students; Teacher aware of the importance of transition and implements strategies that facilitate smooth transitions	Actions of the students are seamless; Students wholly responsible for their actions and teacher overlaps; Teacher seldom behind desk during transitions; Teacher walks among students and incorporates proximity control; Visual and audio reminders are apparent; Little or no loss of instructional time; Motivational devices displayed so students are encouraged to move and get ready quickly; Teacher masterfully facilitates transitions
Classroom Setup	Furniture arranged in a way that is unsafe or impedes accessibility of both teachers and students; Teacher has a hard time getting through desks and	Classroom visibility impaired, but there is a constant rearrangement of desks and other furniture in an effort to ensure that all students can see teacher and board; Classroom generally	Teacher has access to every student; Every student has a way of retrieving necessary materials; Classroom neat and organized; Classroom safe and aisles are clear; Teacher aware of the importance of classroom setup	Furniture arranged for easy movement by both teacher and students. All students have access to each other and to necessary materials even during special activities; Teacher can see all the

Table 7.1 (Continued)

Performance Dimension	Unsatisfactory	Emerging	Proficient	Distinguished
	cubbies when trying to reach a student who needs help; Materials stored in areas where both teachers and students cannot access them easily; Not every student visible to the teacher and vice versa; Room poorly decorated; Classroom untidy and disorganized; Seating arrangement rigid	untidy; Students have a general area to keep their belongings; Classroom generally safe except for clutter and occasional obstacles; Seating arrangement not always followed		students at all times; Students can see teacher and board at all times; Classroom neatly arranged; Materials organized and labeled; Materials in an appropriate location in close proximity to working area of students; Each student has designated area for his or her own personal belongings that is both organized and accessible; Use of space in the classroom maximized
Classroom Atmosphere	Students hesitate to answer and seem tense and anxious; Teacher seems frustrated and tired; Teacher barks instructions and uses lots of criticism and sarcasm; Teacher often threatens to punish students; Teacher inconsistent in discipline procedures; Teacher appears disinterested and uncaring	Some students comfortable but others seem tense; Students are not comfortable with offering their own opinions; Teacher smiles less as the day progresses and is often moody; Teacher compliments and criticizes; Teacher gets frustrated with weaker students; Teacher uses inconsistent	Students generally participate and seem comfortable; Teacher seems satisfied and pleased with the class and her teaching; Teacher uses positive reinforcement most of the time; Teacher generally consistent with discipline procedures; Teacher cares about the students' well-being; Atmosphere appears warm and open	Students supported by teacher; Students motivated to participate and eager to achieve; Students share information and risk giving their opinions voluntarily; Teacher welcomes students enthusiastically in the morning; Teacher gives lots of specific praise; Teacher encourages constantly; Students feel that class is safe and fun; Students appear to trust the teacher;

(Continued)

Table 7.1 (Continued)

Performance Dimension	Unsatisfactory	Emerging	Proficient	Distinguished
		discipline procedures; Teacher shows warmth and care inconsistently; Teacher tries to control her anger; Classroom atmosphere not ideal for learning		Atmosphere open and students can share anything appropriate with teacher and class
Response to Student's Misbehavior	Teacher unaware of what is transpiring most of the time; Teacher often intervenes physically to misbehavior; Teacher screams and sometimes threatens students with punishment; Punishments are unreasonable or inappropriate; Teacher uses humiliation or sarcasm to get the students to listen; Teacher ineffective in dealing with misbehavior	Teacher generally aware of misconduct but unsure what to do; Teacher responds verbally to a misbehavior but doesn't use other strategies; Teacher takes misbehavior personally; Teacher inconsistent in her discipline strategies; Teacher eager to remove students who misbehave; Teacher eager to learn positive strategies but has difficulty implementing them	Teacher alert and usually aware of misbehaviors; Teacher responds to misbehaviors with verbal interventions that are private so as not to embarrass student; Responses to misbehavior appropriate but inconsistent; Teacher addresses the misbehavior, not the character of the student; Teacher develops established rules and procedures; Teacher uses logical consequences; Teacher responds to early signs of misbehavior	Teacher consistent in dealing with misbehavior; Develops a positive approach to classroom management; Remains calm and does not overreact; Clearly states academic and social expectations; Elicits rules and procedures from students; Reacts immediately and positively to misbehavior; Firm, fair, and caring; Develops a systematic approach to classroom management

Table 7.1 (Continued)

Performance Dimension	Unsatisfactory	Emerging	Proficient	Distinguished
Reinforcement	Teacher infrequently uses positive reinforcement techniques; Lacks a systematic approach to reinforcement; Infrequent use of tangible or nontangible reinforcers; Seems uncomfortable or reluctant to use reinforcement	Teacher occasionally uses reinforcement, although inconsistently; Praises students superficially; Reinforces only some students but ignores most others; Lacks training and experience in applying reinforcement	Teacher consistently incorporates reinforcement strategies; Acknowledges most of the students in class every day; Uses names of students most of the time; Provides tangible rewards as soon as appropriate behavior observed; Sends notes home about good behavior; Realizes the importance of reinforcement	Teacher provides constant and consistent reinforcement for positive behavior; All students are acknowledged and reinforced positively; Students have developed, with teacher's assistance, intrinsic motivation; Teacher develops systematic approach to reinforcement; Reinforcement genuine, appropriate, and well distributed
Rules and Procedures	No set routine—different every day; Few set rules; No set consequences; Too much freedom; Children do not know what is expected of them; Rules are stated negatively; No set procedures during transition time; etc.	Too many rules for students to remember; Rules are not posted to remind students; Unrealistic or unreasonable consequences; Rules not elicited and reviewed; Rules not vigorously enforced; Procedures not well-defined; Teacher eager but lacks training and experience	Rules established and reviewed by teacher; Students know what is expected of them; Consequences established and evenly distributed; Students obey rules, even though they may not thoroughly understand them; Rules stated positively; Teacher develops consistent rules and procedures	Rules and procedures are collaboratively established, posted, reviewed, practiced, monitored, and reinforced for all class matters

(Continued)

Table 7.1 (Continued)

Performance Dimension	Unsatisfactory	Emerging	Proficient	Distinguished
Lesson Presentation	Teacher unfamiliar with content/subject; Lesson planning inadequate; Lessons unsuitable for level of class; Lecturing occurs most of the time; Teacher speaks in monotone; Teacher's explanations are vague; Students appear uninterested and off-task; Teacher relies heavily on textbook; Teacher needs training and experience with lesson plan development and presentation	Teacher somewhat familiar with content/subject; Planning evident but has difficulty with delivery; Objectives of lesson are at times unclear; Pacing and delivery problems evident; Students not encouraged to participate; Poor wait time; Inability to project or use voice effectively; Teacher eager but needs additional training and experience	Teacher plans lessons; Goals and objectives stated; Material organized; Students encouraged to participate; Teacher projects her voice and has good pacing; Teacher uses visual aids; Lesson has a clear beginning, middle, and end, and incorporates medial summaries; Teacher communicates lesson well	Lessons well planned, interesting, and meaningful; Teacher incorporates multifaceted approaches and methods to teaching; Teacher uses technology; Teacher projects voice and modulates at appropriate times; Excellent pacing and wait time; Sensitive to learning styles and multiple intelligences; Lesson, altogether very structured, has an introduction, body, conclusion, medial summaries, and reinforcing activities, and is also innovative; Students' level of understanding monitored well; Clearly, a master teacher.

164

DEALING WITH ADMINISTRATIVE EXIGENCIES: THE ROLE OF THE AP IN THE SCHOOL CAFETERIA AND FOR SCHOOL SECURITY

RESPOND

What factors are important to consider for an indoor lunch period? What factors are important in organizing a school safety plan? Record your responses below detailing specific areas of responsibility in terms of the role of the AP, logistical concerns, personnel, problem areas, and so on. Then compare your responses to the two outlines that follow.

_____

_____

_____

_____

_____

_____

_____

_____

_____

_____

_____

_____

_____

_____

_____

_____

Here is an activity you'll likely have to deal with on a daily basis that was rarely, if ever, addressed in your graduate courses: How to run an effective lunch period. Imagine having to supervise a cafeteria filled with 200 youngsters on an inclement day during indoor lineup. Many of you don't have to imagine because you face that dreaded activity regularly. Below you will find an outline of key ideas and areas of responsibilities for effective administration of the lunch period. Following this is an outline related to the role of an AP in school safety. Peruse the outlines below and compare your responses in the previous response activity.

The Role of the AP in the School Cafeteria

Participant in Formulating Policy

1. Grade levels and number of students to be programmed for lunch periods

2. Cafeteria environment: size, location, resources

3. Routines: entrance, seating, serving, dismissal

4. Staffing: personnel on duty

5. Passes to bathroom, library, and other places

6. Indoor versus outdoor lunch

7. "Captive lunch" or leaving building (eating outside or going home)

8. After-lunch activities: music, games, socializing, sports

When developing policies for cafeteria procedures, be sure to include others, including teachers, cafeteria staff, and other school administrators. Brief the principal on your plan, asking for feedback and suggestions.

Problems Involved in Cafeteria Supervision

1. Developing a plan for cafeteria duty: problem solving, proactive strategies, personnel, resources, emergency plan

2. Disturbances (individual or group) or riots: plan of action

3. Dealing with intruders, cutters, and so on.

4. Student dissatisfaction with cafeteria conditions (e.g., prices, menus and food preparation, waiting in lines)

5. Cafeteria traffic, passes, dismissal and entrance routines, and so on.

6. Crowd control

7. Conflict between students in cafeteria, between students and cafeteria personnel, or school staff members

8. Conflict between cafeteria personnel and custodial personnel on clean-up duties

Periodically, you should meet with your cafeteria committee to review problems that have arisen. What measures could be taken to minimize future incidents? What other measures can be taken to deal with similar problems in the future?

The AP's Responsibilities

Teacher Personnel

1. Selection, training, and supervision of coordinators

2. Training and supervision of assigned personnel

3. Rotation of personnel

4. Assignment of posts

5. Clarification of duties

6. Training in control of students

Interface With All Personnel Including Custodians, Cafeteria Personnel, School Aides, Security Aides, Dietician, etc.

Students

1. Control and discipline

2. Service squad comprised of outstanding students

3. Student cafeteria committee (to make recommendations for improvement)

4. Drug problems

5. Lavatories: supervision, passes, controls

6. Need for constructive educational activities

Community Complaints and Requests; Parent Involvement and Cooperation

Cafeteria duty is certainly not one of the more pleasant chores of APs. However, running a smooth, efficient, and effective lunch duty is essential. Poorly run lunch periods can endanger the safety of students and others and can have a deleterious effect on the rest of the school day. If chaos, for instance, reigns supreme during lunchtime, carryover will occur in the classrooms after lunch. Use the general guidelines mentioned previously to develop a plan that fits your needs. Review your plan with your committee and then monitor the plan carefully as you begin the implementation stage. I also suggest you visit some other schools that have efficient cafeteria operations to cull some ideas for your own school.

The Role of the AP in School Security and Safety

Although the principal is chiefly responsible and accountable for the safety of all school personnel and students, an AP may be assigned responsibility for school security and safety.

Responsibility of the AP in Matters of Safety

1. Ensure compliance with rules and regulations for maintenance of public order on school property

2. Supervise safety personnel under her or his jurisdiction

3. Implement a school safety plan

4. Update the school safety plan yearly to reflect changing problems and conditions in the school

5. Establish rules and procedures for visitors

Establish a committee to develop a school safety plan. Ensure that everyone's responsibilities are clear. Meet often at the start, then regularly throughout the year, even when no incidents occur. Be proactive, not reactive. Anticipate problems and develop contingency plans.

School Security and Safety

1. Supervision of school guards

2. Contacts with community and city agencies

3. Organization and operation of fire and shelter drills

4. Coordinate with police department

You may not be able to do all this yourself. Encourage support and assistance from committee members and even parent volunteers.

Creation of Desirable School Climate

1. Develop, disseminate, and analyze results of a schoolwide school climate survey

2. Utilize results to improve relationships between students and administration, faculty and parents, parents and administration, and so on.

3. Involvement of parents, students, school personnel, and community in formulation of school policies

Developing an action research study here is a good idea. Utilize the school leadership team or whatever committee is at your disposal to administer a school climate survey. Committee members can gather, analyze, and interpret data. As committee chair, you should be integrally involved every step of the way. Use survey results to improve the security plan. Disseminate results and invite responses from the school community.

Preparation for Emergencies

1. Help plan and implement a school safety/emergency plan

2. Coordinate with custodial staff safety regulations including checking of all fire extinguishers

3. Develop plan for false alarms

4. Written instruction for all drills including floor marshals, coverage of posts, and so on

5. Procedures to be followed in case of accidents (emergency contact cards completed for all personnel and students, police contact, parent notification, etc.)

6. First aid instructions posted, staff trained in CPR, contact with school nurse or local hospital officials

Emergencies will occur. Anticipate the varied types of emergencies and develop appropriate measures to deal with them. Constantly review procedures.

Special Rooms

1. Shops (signs on walls, written instructions to pupils, safety tests of all equipment, alertness to hazardous conditions, licensed teachers only, regulations for safety posted on walls, etc.)

2. Gymnasiums (check room, equipment properly spaced, storage of equipment, etc.)

3. Science Rooms, Laboratories, Storage Rooms (condition of equipment, storage of flammable materials, licensed teacher for demonstrations of potential hazards, etc.)

Once a week, take a walk around the school with key committee members to look for potential "hot spots." Check room conditions (e.g., cracked ceilings, leaky pipes, etc.). Check grounds and surrounding neighborhood as well.

Flow of Traffic

1. Clearly labeled staircases

2. Special directions

3. Special instructions for elevator use

4. Hall coverage

5. Routines for walking in halls

6. Security assigned and on duty

7. Routine for use of school buses (deployment of personnel to avoid accidents from oncoming traffic and from bus movements)

8. Arrival and dismissal procedures

Review procedures with committee members every month. Solicit input and recommendations for improvement.

Additional Student Regulations

1. Constant supervision

2. No students leave the building without permission

3. Window safety in classrooms and hallways

Conduct assemblies to review security issues with students. Involve students on security committees.

Relationship With Custodians

1. Fast channel of communication

2. Prompt service if hazards are noticed

3. Repairs where necessary

4. Established precautions for inclement weather (snow removal, rubber mats for entrance, etc.)

Develop positive relationships with custodial staff. Include them on important committees and solicit their input. Their perspective is unique and invaluable. They'll appreciate your attentiveness and willingness to include them in these important matters.

School Plant

1. Monitoring entrances

2. Separate late door and personnel post

3. Empty rooms locked

4. Special locks for rooms with machines or equipment

5. Special doors for computer labs, and so on

6. Keys

Again, conduct walk-arounds, checking indoors and outside at least every week or even more often if needed.

Protection Against Intruders or Violence

1. No person admitted unless on legitimate business

2. All school personnel and students should have appropriate visible IDs

3. Instructions to staff when a suspected intruder is seen

4. Deployment of a security force to provide for maximum security at all times

5. Available list of emergency numbers—precinct, fire marshal, patrol officers, and so on

6. Police contacted quickly in case of emergency

7. Firm and swift action against intruders

8. Precinct notified when dismissal times are changed, evening meetings scheduled, and afterschool events scheduled

Conduct role plays to deal with intruders. Hold debriefing sessions with committee members. Review what went well and what may need improvement. Again, proactivity is key.

Money and Other Valuables

1. Money to bank daily

2. School safe to house valuables and cash

3. Oversee school funds

4. Control of all keys and master keys

5. Instructions for staff regarding storage of personal valuables

6. Locker safety

7. Student orientation regarding bringing money and valuables to school and other personal property

Disseminate to school staff procedures regarding valuables. Disseminate information verbally and in written memo form.

Other Real-Life Scenarios: What Would You Do?

Read the recollection that follows as an example that they really can never teach you about in graduate school.

RECOLLECTION

I recall my interview for the assistant principalship. As I entered the large conference room at the local district office, I recalled the admonition from a colleague who told me several days earlier to "relax because the word out is that the interim acting AP in the school has the job anyway." I had actually heard this rumor from several others in the district. I was resigned to the notion that I would use this experience as a testing ground since this would be my first such interview. Nevertheless, I was anxious when my name was called and I entered the room. Seated around a rectangular table in a nicely decorated room containing various artifacts from a recent multicultural fair, were the school superintendent, the teacher's union rep, the supervisor's association rep, two teachers, and three parent representatives. I noticed that the principal wasn't there. His absence confirmed the rumors that he had already selected his interim AP.

The questioning began and I responded to the various questions as my answers were recorded into a tape recorder. I felt kind of relaxed and enjoyed showcasing my ideas for school improvement. I talked about working collegially with teachers and discussed my ideas for dealing with recalcitrant students. The 29-minute interview passed by rather quickly. The superintendent thanked me and I left the room.

The district's policy for AP interviews was well-known. After the first round a candidate is usually chosen. To my surprise, I received a call a few weeks later for a second interview. "What was this all about?" I wondered. "Hey, what do I have to lose?" As I entered the interview room once again, I noticed most of the same people seated around the table with one exception. The principal was there this time. The interview proceeded without incident. After fielding about ten questions, I wondered when and if the principal would ask me a question. In fact, his demeanor at the interview was like a reluctant student seated outside the dean's office. His back was half-turned away as if disinterested by the whole process. I was too anxious to take much notice though.

The superintendent then asked the principal, "Do you have a question for Dr. Glanz?" He turned around in his seat and looked at me. His penetrating eyes were as fearsome as his 6'6" ? stature. "What would you do if a boy pissed in the school yard during lunch?" I was stunned. "Pissed in the school yard?" I had learned many things in my graduate classes about instructional

(Continued)

(Continued)

leadership, team management, learning communities, and curriculum development, but never had we discussed a child "pissing" in a school yard.

Incredulous, I paused a moment hoping to hear him say that he was joking. But he looked as stern and serious as he was when he posed the question. I could sense the irritation and near embarrassment by the body language of the superintendent. I decided to respond. I said something about not embarrassing the child but that I would see him privately to ask him why he acted that way in an attempt to understand his inappropriate behavior, etc., etc.

Inside a few days, to my astonishment, I received a call from the district office that I had been selected AP at P.S. X. I was elated. I had attained my aspiration of serving as an AP.

What lessons can I relate to you, my reader, from this very true experience? First, never listen to rumors about a position being filled. Sure, there was an interim acting AP, but I later found out that the principal didn't like her. Why was the principal absent at the first interview? I discovered that he didn't like the superintendent either and didn't show up to irritate him and force a second interview. Second, expect the unexpected!

What would you do if while on lunch duty you see a child "piss" in the school yard on the fence in sight of many children?

APs deal with many other realistic issues besides lunch duty and school safety issues. Below are real-life scenarios. They all have one thing in common, that is, you likely didn't discuss them in graduate school. What would you do?

1. A parent calls you and accuses Mr. Henderson of hitting her child. She demands that you immediately dismiss the teacher. She doesn't like your response and threatens to come up to school to shoot you. (You think this would never happen? Think again; it happened to a colleague of mine.)

   _____

   _____

   _____

   _____

   _____

   _____

   _____

2. During an outdoor lunch period, a boy sustains a deep cut on his leg and is bleeding profusely. You happen on the scene. Describe in step-by-step fashion what you would do.

_____

_____

_____

_____

_____

3. The number of accidents in the school yard at lunchtime has increased dramatically. Indicate two immediate steps you would take and two recommendations you would make to the principal for dealing with accidents in the yard. State how each recommendation would contribute to safety in the yard.

_____

_____

_____

_____

_____

4. You receive a complaint from parents via the telephone and letter about the incidence of pediculosis (head lice) that appears to be spreading rapidly throughout the school. Some parents are very angry because their children become affected again after their condition has been cleared up. State four recommendations for immediate action you would make to the principal concerning the problem of pediculosis.

_____

_____

_____

_____

_____

5. A food fight breaks out during an indoor lunch lineup. You shout over the loudspeaker to no avail. Three lunch aids have not shown up yet. You are alone in the room with nearly 200 children, and about 15 of them are now throwing food.

_____

_____

_____

_____

(Continued)

(Continued)

6. The principal tells you that there are no existing rules and procedures when you coordinate lunch duty. What rules and procedures would you develop for lunchroom behavior? What happens if students do not comply with the rules?

_____

_____

_____

_____

_____

_____

7. A teacher reports that her purse is missing. It is 5 minutes prior to dismissal. She tells you she intends to strip-search the students. Then she hangs up the phone.

_____

_____

_____

_____

_____

_____

8. Your secretary receives an anonymous call that there is a bomb in the building.

_____

_____

_____

_____

_____

_____

9. You catch a custodian drinking alcohol on duty in the basement.

_____

_____

_____

_____

_____

_____

10. Children are bored during indoor lunch lineups. What varied activities can you plan to keep their attention and minimize misbehavior?

_____

_____

_____

_____

_____

Other Issues Rarely Addressed

Below are four unrelated areas of concern raised by many APs. Suggestions are offered. Realize, of course, that many other approaches may be warranted. Also, note that a plethora of other issues were probably never addressed in graduate school. Experience will be the best teacher. Learn from more experienced APs, and always keep an open mind.

Developing a Master Schedule

- Practice using a mock schedule. Your school is K–5 with two classes per grade level. Twelve teachers in total each must be scheduled for lunch, a preparation period, and a period in which a cluster (art, music, or physical education) teacher takes the class (one period a day). For instance, the art teacher takes them on Mondays, the music teacher on Wednesdays, and the physical education teacher on Fridays. Considering an eight-period day (no block scheduling), develop a schedule. What other information might you need to know to proceed?
- Seek advice from an experienced AP. That's what I did when my principal asked me to develop the schoolwide schedule for the upcoming year.
- Gather all necessary information. Collect last year's schedule, teacher requests, room allocations, student lists, and so on.
- Ask the principal for advice. Solicit input from the principal.
- Develop the schedule while away from school. In my case the principal gave me two days off. In the quiet of my apartment, I was undisturbed and able to give full attention to this tedious assignment.
- Use 3 × 5 index cards, and lay them out on a large table. Record all information on a master sheet as you go along. At the end of the process compare information on the index cards with the master sheet.

- Double- and triple-check everything. After the first draft is completed, review the schedule, looking for conflicts and other problems. Invite a friend or colleague to look it over as well. Even ask a teacher in your school to preview the schedule before mass dissemination.
- Attend a workshop. Although I learned the hard way (by myself), I'd recommend you attend a training session either at a conference or at the district office. Perhaps a more experienced AP can tutor you as well.

The AP's Role in Special Education

- Demonstrate an inclusive attitude toward all students enrolled in the building that flows down through the faculty and student population.
- Foster special education students' involvement in extracurricular and cocurricular activities.
- Seek ways to highlight accomplishments of all students and to give recognition and praise.
- Encourage building-level personnel to use the building administrator as a "reward" to share in good news and accomplishments rather than "bad news" only. (Sometimes the building level administrator is the only person of authority beyond the classroom teacher with whom the special education student has an opportunity to develop a positive relationship.
- Encourage building-level personnel with instructional/supervisory responsibility for special education students to communicate with the building administrator and CSE (Committee on Special Education, or whatever it's called in your location) personnel in a timely fashion concerning specific student needs or issues.
- Encourage parental communication with building administrators. Open communication can serve to minimize or ameliorate the need for due process action by parents unhappy with special education services provided and serves as a support system for the CSE.
- Serve as a resource for faculty contemplating referral to the CSE of an at-risk student so that referral becomes the last step in an exploratory process when need arises and not the first step—as per least restrictive environment philosophy.
- Ensure the attendance and participation of required building level personnel and classroom teacher(s), special education teacher (if in addition to classroom teacher—i.e., resource room), specialists (OT, PT, speech, etc.) in IEP meetings by arranging for substitute coverage, if needed, and taking action if any teacher or specialist refuses to attend.

Strategies for Running Effective Meetings

- Develop a purpose. A meeting should have a goal and a series of clear objectives.
- Draft an agenda. Sequence topics to be discussed.
- Prepare handouts and materials. Plan and prepare everything in advance.
- Review the agenda with an experienced AP or principal. Solicit input and suggestions from others.
- Keep to the agenda when conducting the meeting.
- Solicit input from all participants.
- Monitor self-talk. Don't dominate conversations.
- Purchase the best small book on the subject currently available: *Energize Your Meetings With Laughter* by Feigelson (ASCD).

Methods for Involving Parents

- Remain accessible to parents. Greet them every day. Begin conversations on mundane matters to start. Demonstrate your care and willingness to listen to them.
- Personally invite parents. Invite selected parents to attend a workshop or join a committee.
- Start a "take a picture with your child" campaign. Once parents are in the school invite them to join a committee, and so on.
- Institute a telephone and e-mail "hotline" for parents. Parents will appreciate these innovative ways to receive information daily about their child and about school programs.
- Institute a "Meet With the Assistant Principal Night" at which you can discuss general policies and possible ways of involving parents on curriculum committees.
- Ask yourself every day (or at least every other day), "Have I spoken to a parent today to solicit involvement in some aspect of the school?" Don't always focus on parents whom you contact for student misbehavior. Actually, be proactive. Call a parent to invite her or him for discussion. Offer concrete ideas on how they can assist, even if they work full-time.

IN-BASKET SIMULATION

1. Two secretaries, Ms. Rodriguez and Ms. Haley, are in constant conflict over their duties. The principal asks you to handle the situation. Set forth and justify the steps you would take to resolve the

(Continued)

(Continued)

situation. (Here are some possible solutions: Listen to both sides; meet with each secretary separately and bring them together only if a reasonable resolution is possible; chastise as necessary, verbally and/or in writing; monitor future activity closely; develop and implement professional rules and procedures; etc.)

2. Your principal asks you to be responsible for school photographs. Describe how you handle this responsibility. (Here are some possible solutions: Find out if a policy exists or how a former AP dealt with the situation; form a committee for ideas and assistance; consult Chapter 6 for other ideas; etc.)

3. Teachers in your middle school have complained that the dean awards treats to students sent to his office for disciplinary action. They complain to you, the AP, that such rewards reinforce student misbehavior. The teachers demand action. What would you do? (Here are some possible solutions: Investigate the matter by observing and then speaking with the dean; explain the teachers' perspective and ask the dean for suggestions without accusing her or him; monitor behavior and intercede as necessary; etc.)

4. As a middle school AP sitting in your office speaking to a parent, you receive a phone call from a lunchroom aid who implores you, "Please come to the cafeteria as fast as you can. All the students are shouting that the food is terrible and some are throwing their food and trays on the floor. We can't control them." Describe your immediate and long-term actions. (Here are some possible solutions: Realize the emergency and tell the parent you'll try to return as soon as possible; reschedule the meeting with the parent; learn the difference between something that is urgent and something that is important [see Recollection in Chapter 2]; etc.)

5. You are an AP in a school where aides are on patrol some periods during the day. The principal asks you to write a circular on procedures that should be followed. List the procedures and suggestions you would include. Select one major problem they are likely to encounter and set forth the instructions you would give them to handle the situation. (Answers may vary.)

6. As an AP you receive this e-mail from a parent: "Dear Mr. X, My son Douglas is in Ms. Treacher's class. Yesterday, two boys in his class, Sam F. and Richard F., asked him for five dollars on the way home

from school. Douglas told them he didn't have any money. They said they would beat him up if he didn't bring them the money today. I am keeping Douglas home until I can ensure his safety. Yours truly, Mrs. Jackson." Describe your actions in detail. (I'll leave this one for you, as I will the next one. Share responses with a colleague.)

7. Describe the actions you would take in each of these situations that were probably not addressed in grad school:
   a. Experienced teachers complain about having to do lesson plans.
   b. Faculty complain that grade conferences are a waste of time.
   c. The fifth and sixth grades are unruly on their way back to the main building after lunch.
   d. The fourth floor's LCD projector and laptop are missing.
   e. A new teacher sends a misbehaving student to your office without informing you.
   f. Two students set fire to the wastepaper basket outside your office.
   g. A teacher is accused by students of telling them the answers on the standardized reading test.
   h. A passionate fight breaks out between two ninth-grade girls just as you are passing them in the hallway.

8

Do I Want to Remain an Assistant Principal?

The forgotten man . . . is frequently the assistant principal. We know he is there but little about him.

—William L. Pharis, *National Association of Elementary School Principals*

◆

FOCUS QUESTIONS

1. What do you enjoy most about serving as an AP?

2. What are your greatest challenges?

3. Do you see the assistant principalship as a career-long position? Why or why not?

4. Do you think the assistant principalship is good training ground for the principalship?

5. What advice would you give APs about their careers?

6. How are APs and principals portrayed in the media? See the Recollection following in this chapter.

Many view the assistant principalship as a stepping-stone to the principalship. There are two problems with this view. Studies, many of which that have been cited in this book, demonstrate that duties and responsibilities of APs are at times so different from those of principals that the assistant principalship does not provide appropriate training for becoming a principal (see, e.g., Gorton & Kettman, 1985; Koru, 1993). Second, the assistant principalship should be viewed as a unique and valuable career position in its own right (Pellicer & Stevenson, 1991). *The Assistant Principal's Handbook* has been premised on the idea that the assistant principalship is a worthy and professional career position in its own right. The deployment of APs as mere disciplinarians and lunchroom coordinators, if not attendants, seriously erodes a valuable leadership resource in a school. Framed as such, the assistant principalship provides few incentives for persons to enter the position and, perhaps more important, to remain an AP.

REFLECT

Why did you become an AP? Why have you remained an AP? Do you aspire to the principalship?

_____

_____

_____

_____

_____

The Assistant Principal's Handbook has stressed that APs should be involved in instructional, supervisory, and curricular leadership. APs inevitably must deal with administrative exigencies and disciplinary matters, but not as the primary focus of their work. Conceived as such, the assistant principalship is somewhat related to the principalship. Certainly, principals are involved in other matters beyond the duties and responsibilities of APs. APs who seek to assume the principalship need additional training.

Form 8.1   Respond

Article I. RESPOND				
SA = Strongly Agree ("For the most part, yes") *A = Agree ("Yes, but . . .")* *D = Disagree ("No, but . . .")* *SD = Strongly Disagree ("For the most part, no")*	*SA*	*A*	*D*	*SD*
1. I definitely know I want to remain an AP.				
2. I definitely know I aspire to the principalship.				
3. I don't really want all the responsibility that comes with the principalship.				
4. I usually like assisting rather than formulating school policy.				
5. My friends and colleagues urge me to become a principal.				
6. I am influenced by my friends and colleagues and will likely strive to become a principal.				
7. I have a mentor as an AP or principal.				
8. I am a lifelong learner, and I regularly read journals, attend conferences, and seek to improve my skills in my position.				
9. I am proud of my position.				
10. I aspire for a position beyond the principalship.				

Some suggestions for those readers interested in remaining APs and for those interested in pursuing the principalship follow.

Remaining an AP

- Be proud of your position. An AP is in a position to accomplish much for the school organization. You are still close enough to the students to be involved with them on a daily basis. Remaining compassionate toward students and passionate about your work with teachers are worthy endeavors.

- Continue to learn. Many of you have learned to perform on the job. Yet, as you very well know, there is so much to know and accomplish. Continue to read literature in your field by reading education magazines, journals, and attending conferences such as the annual meeting of the Association for Supervision and Curriculum Development (ASCD), among others.

- Identify a "pet" project and assume leadership. APs have much to offer and can accomplish many things because of their position in schools and availability of resources at their disposal. Take leadership in a special area of concern for the school, such as providing ongoing staff development in literacy, organizing a study group for low achievers, or forming parent partnerships to raise funds for your grade. You will certainly become enthusiastic as you carve a niche, so to speak, for yourself in the school and/or community, and at the same time you will provide for leadership in a much needed area. Always, of course, consult with and inform the principal (see suggestions later for working with your principal).

- Enjoy the job. After several years in the position, people may naturally ask you the following question: "So when are you going to become a principal?" Explain to them that you are happy as an AP and state boldly that at this time you don't strive for the principalship. Your duties are challenging and you enjoy remaining close to the students. Providing instructional leadership, for instance, to teachers is very rewarding, and there is much to accomplish.

Pursuing the Principalship

- Continue to learn. There is certainly nothing wrong in wanting to become a principal. In fact, for those gifted individuals who truly aspire to accomplish much good for a school, becoming a principal is a worthy goal. We need talented leaders in the principalship. Working as a principal, however, is in many respects unlike the work of an AP. You are now as principal ultimately responsible for everything and everyone in the school building. Along with greater responsibility and accountability come broader responsibilities. Therefore, principals must continually extend their knowledge and skill base beyond their graduate study. Attending conferences, reading journals, and even taking additional courses (e.g., going for a doctorate) will contribute to a heightened sense of professionalism and expertise.

- Seek a mentor. Although relevant for APs, this suggestion is even more critical for aspiring principals. Principals at times rise to the position after several years as an AP. Still, some become principals without first assuming an assistant principalship. Regardless, find someone you can confide in and to serve as a mentor. Relying on someone you respect and look up to is very important not only for training for the position but also for someone you can rely on and call upon in times of crises.

Suggestions for Working With Your Principal

Here are some commonsense tips for working with your principal:

- Realize that you are her or his "assistant," and as such you are there to carry out her or his policies and to take leadership responsibilities in the areas she or he delegates to you.
- Protect and support your principal.
- Understand and accommodate your principal's leadership style.
- Remain assertive by requesting to assume leadership responsibilities in special areas.
- Do not make any major decision without seeking the assistance and/or advice of your principal.
- Remain honest by openly sharing your views of instructional improvement with your principal.
- Never criticize or question the authority of your principal in public.
- Offer to assist your principal in instructional, curricular, and administrative matters.
- Understand your principal's strengths and limitations, and offer to assist where and when necessary.
- Remain steadfast in your beliefs and share them with your principal.
- Seek advice from your principal.
- Offer to cover a lunch duty or some other mundane administrative assignment from time to time.
- Offer concrete proposals to maximize instructional staff performance.
- Share teacher views with the principal.
- Seek, in private, a rationale for your principal's decisions.
- Remember that although your allegiance and loyalty remain with the principal, you are ultimately responsible to the parents and children you serve.

RECOLLECTION

I recall watching a made-for-TV movie called Kidz in the Woods that portrayed an AP in an unpleasant light. The movie was about a dedicated history teacher (played by Dave Thomas) who takes eight academically and emotionally troubled high school students on a summer class trip during which they retrace the Oregon Trail via wagon trains. The object of the exercise is to "show how yesterday's events can help solve today's problems." The principal, against this unorthodox experiment, is portrayed as an autocrat, a bureaucrat, and, ultimately, a dimwit. The vice principal, playing a vital role in the movie, is also depicted in various negative ways, at least during most of the movie. This film also demonstrates an interesting and not uncommon relationship between a male principal and a female vice principal.

Mr. Henry Dunbar, a middle-aged conservative high school principal, confirms his role as petty bureaucrat when he chastises renegade history teacher Mr. Foster, who is the main character in this amusing movie. Dunbar calls Foster into his office and demands that he follow the prescribed curriculum. "What's obvious to me is that you blame me because I insist you follow my standard curriculum." "Your standard curriculum," Foster retorts, "is substandard, and I blame you for not accepting the responsibility for teaching these kids more than is in their books." Foster proceeds to leave Dunbar's office as the bell rings. "I gotta go . . . unless of course you want to teach my class." Dunbar remains silent. The principal's incompetence is not too subtlety inferred. The image as incompetent bureaucrat is effectively communicated. In a later scene, the vice principal is similarly portrayed as having little, if any, teaching experience. At a school board meeting, Vice Principal Felicia Duffy defends her experience by asserting, "I did teach . . . for several semesters, that is." (What does that mean to tell us about APs?)

Mr. Dunbar, determined to waylay Foster's efforts at succeeding with his innovative strategies, demands that his vice principal, Miss Duffy, videotape the class trip as students inevitably get into trouble. Armed with this documentation, Dunbar can convince the Board that he was right. Miss Duffy, aghast at the principal's deceit and unethical behavior, tries to convince her boss not to pursue this campaign. Relying on his superordinate position in the school hierarchy and employing an autocratic tactic, Dunbar tells Duffy, "You, unlike Foster, don't have tenure." Duffy reluctantly is coerced to comply. Interestingly, Duffy, as vice principal, complies with the chicanery rather than maintaining her integrity by adhering to more ethical standards of behavior. The image of the principal as dimwit is ultimately imparted as Dunbar's plan is foiled. Principals are portrayed negatively as compared to more idealistic, intelligent teachers.

How is the vice principal portrayed? How do media influence public perceptions of school administrators? What about the effect on us as APs ? (see Glanz, 1998, for more detail)

IN-BASKET SIMULATION

1. You have been an AP in a K–six elementary school for six years. The principal calls you into his office one morning and claims that you are undermining his position in the school, especially with teachers and parents, and that he has heard you say, "I want his job." (Possible responses include: Be honest—confirm or deny the rumors; demonstrate your loyalty to the principal by word and deed; inform the principal that you will speak with parents; etc.)

2. You have been an AP for ten years and are content in the position. The superintendent calls you one afternoon and offers you the principalship of a newly built school in the district. She says, "You have served as an exemplary AP for so many years. I want you to lead this new school." (Possible responses include: Be honest with yourself and the superintendent (do you want the job?); decline politely, reaffirming your dedication to the school/district; thank the superintendent for her confidence in you, and tell her you'll consider the offer and get back to her in two days; etc.)

3.   You are asked by your spouse, "Do you want to remain an AP, or do you aspire for the principalship?" (Answers will vary.)

Resource A: Annotated Bibliography

There is no friend as loyal as a book.

—Ernest Hemingway

The following list is not meant to serve as a comprehensive resource by any means. The titles I have selected to annotate are few but, in my opinion, are among the most useful references for assistant principals. I may have missed, of course, many other important works. Nevertheless, the list below is a good start. Don't forget that life is a long journey of continuous learning. Continue to hone your skills by reading good books and articles on the topic. No one is ever perfect, and everyone can learn something new by keeping current with the literature in the field. Share your readings and reactions with a colleague.

Black, J. A., & English, F. W. (1986). *What they don't tell you in schools of education about school administration.* Lancaster, PA: Technomic.

Classic treatise for coping with school politics—includes career suggestions

Blasé, J., & Blasé, J. (2002). *Handbook of instructional leadership.* Thousand Oaks, CA: Corwin Press.

Comprehensive study of how instructional supervision is actually practiced and how it affects teachers—practical

Calabrese, R. L., & Zepeda, S. J. (1997). *The reflective supervisor: A practical guide for educators.* Larchmont, NY: Eye on Education.

Packed with practical strategies for effective practice

Danielson, C. (1996). *Enhancing professional practice: A framework for teaching.* Alexandria, VA: Association for Supervision and Curriculum Development.

A framework or model for understanding teaching based on current research in the field

Glanz, J. (2000). *Relax for success: A practical guide for educators to relieve stress.* Norwood, MA: Christopher-Gordon.
    Useful resource for dealing with stress—comes with a CD-ROM

Glatthorn, A. A. (1997). *Differentiated supervision* (2nd ed.). Alexandria, VA: Association for Supervision and Curriculum Development.
    Small book that is theoretically grounded and practically sound—helps you develop a supervisory and evaluative system suited to your school's needs

Glickman, C. D. (2002). *Leadership for learning: How to help teachers succeed.* Alexandria, VA: Association for Supervision and Curriculum Development.
    Comprehensive yet quick guide to practical instructional leadership strategies—great list of resources

Gronlund, N. E. (2003). *Assessment of student achievement* (7th ed.). Boston: Allyn & Bacon.
    Clearest, most concise work on the subject

Koehler, M. (1999). *Administrator's staff development activities kit.* San Francisco: Jossey-Bass.
    Ready-to-use teaching materials for training, supervision, and evaluation—reproducible forms—great for inservice

Mamchak, P. S., & Mamchak, S. R. (1998). *Encyclopedia of school letters.* San Francisco: Jossey-Bass.
    Packed with sample memos and letters in many areas APs would find useful

Meyer, H. E. (1992). *Lifetime encyclopedia of letters.* Englewood Cliffs, NJ: Prentice Hall.
    Valuable resource to write letters: requesting favors, declining requests, fundraising, providing info, dealing with complaints, letters expressing sympathy and condolences, congratulations, other business letters, and so on

Ramsey, R. D. (1996). *The principal's book of lists.* San Francisco: Jossey-Bass.
    Useful lists—a nuts-and-bolts with lots of info—tips, even for APs

Simpson, P. R. (2000). *Assistant principal's survival guide: Practical guidelines and materials for managing all areas of your work.* Paramus, NJ: Prentice Hall.

Time-saving resource jam-packed with techniques for virtually every aspect of school administration. Although short on instructional strategies for APs, this is a practical treatise that includes more than forty reproducible letters, forms, and reports useful to some APs.

Weller, L. D., & Weller, S. J. (2002). *The assistant principal: Essentials for effective leadership.* Thousand Oaks, CA: Corwin Press.

Guidebook and training manual on leadership—deals with politics, communication skills, instructional improvement, and staff development

Resource B: Web Resources for Assistant Principals

F ew, if any, good sites are devoted solely to APs. Following are some of the better resources on the Web related to instructional and teaching issues. I offer them as suggestions because the voluminous material that exists can actually turn you off. Few of us know where or how to begin. You will find the following sites enormously helpful.

www.cybertext.net.au/tct2002/tutorials/section5.htm
> Offers many links for school leaders

http://nt.watauga.k12.nc.us/whs/wonders/admin.htm
> Nice Web site for school administrators

www.aasa.org/
> American Association of School Administrators

www.naesp.org/
> National Association of Elementary School Principals

www.nassp.org/
> National Association of Secondary School Principals

www.ed.gov
> The U.S. Department of Education Web site

www.teachers.net/lessons/search.html
> This site enables you to search a lesson plan exchange (K–12).

www.teachers.net/c1gi-bin/lessons/sort.cgi
> Lesson plans at this site are sorted by category.

www.glavac.com
> Busy educator's guide to the World Wide Web

www.k-6educators.about.com
> Offers links for elementary educators

www.yahoo.com/Education/K_12
> Offers links to reference materials

www.new-teacher.com
> A site for new teachers and student teachers

www.discoveryschool.com/schrockguide
> Kathy Schrock's Guide for Educators is a categorized list of sites on the Internet found to be useful for enhancing curriculum and teacher professional growth. It is updated daily.

www.teachernet.com
> Smart Ideas for Busy Teachers

www.AtoZteacherstuff.com
> Online lesson plans

www.NAEYC.org
> National Association for the Education of Young Children

www.google.com
> Great advice: search Google by typing in "classroom management"—now, spend the day exploring. (Also, try typing in "discipline," although many nonschool discipline sites are included; you'll have to pick and choose. It's worth exploring though. Google is accessible, easy-to-use, and current.)

www.masterteacher.com
> This for-profit Web site is a phenomenal storehouse of educational resources (some for free) that include videos and books on a host of relevant topics (e.g., leadership, inclusion, mentoring, etc.)—a must to browse with loads of teaching ideas. Subscribe for free materials. Great free catalog; 1-800-669-9633

http://soupserver.com
> Daily inspirational sayings—uplifts the soul

www.newteachercenter.org
>   Promotes excellence and diversity in schools—very teacher friendly

www.alfiekohn.org
>   Useful site packed with the ideas and writings of a noted critic of public education

www.effectiveteaching.com
>   Harry Wong's site—packed with info

www.pdkintl.org
>   National organization of immense influence

www.proteacher.com and www.innovativeclassroom.com
>   Both sites contain many useful ideas and tools (including lesson plans in content areas) on a variety of educational topics—easy to navigate

www.splcenter.org
>   Tolerance and diversity issues

Consult *Educational Leadership ASCD journal—"Web Wonders"*: www.ascd.org
>   Great resources on a plethora of topics

www.school.discovery.com/schrockguide/assess.html
>   An impressive list of resources related to assessment

www.lessonplanspage.com
>   More than 1,000 lessons plans K–12

www.askeric.org/virtual/lessons
>   Lesson plans by topic and grade level

Also see Susan Brooks-Youngs's *101 Best Web Sites for Principals.* Eugene, OR: International Society for Technology in Education, 2003.

References

Acheson, K. A., & Gall, M. D. (1997). *Techniques in the clinical supervision of teachers.* New York: Longman.

Balliet, T. M. (1891). Discussion of Anderson's paper. *National Educational Association Proceedings, 32,* 365–379.

Beach, D. M., & Reinhartz, J. (2000). *Supervisory leadership: Focus on instruction.* Boston: Allyn & Bacon.

Blasé, J., & Blasé, J. (1998). *Handbook of instructional leadership.* Thousand Oaks, CA: Corwin Press.

Blasé, J., & Blasé, J. (2002). *Empowering teachers: What successful principals do* (2nd ed.). Thousand Oaks, CA: Corwin Press.

Bransford, J. D., Brown, A. L., & Cocking, R. R. (Eds.). (1999). *How people learn: Brain, mind, experience, and school.* Washington, DC: National Academy Press.

Calabrese, R. L. (1991). Effective assistant principals: What do they do? *NASSP Bulletin, 75,* 51–57.

Calabrese, R. L., Short, G., & Zepeda, S. J. (1996). *Hands-on leadership tools for principals.* Princeton, NJ: Eye on Education.

Calabrese, R. L., & Tucker-Ladd, P. R. (1991). The principal and assistant principal: A mentoring relationship. *NASSP Bulletin, 75,* 64–74.

Canter, L. (1989). *Assertive discipline for secondary school teachers: Inservice video package and leader's manual.* Santa Monica, CA: Lee Canter and Associates.

Carnegie Forum on Education and the Economy. (1986). *A nation prepared: Teachers for the twenty-first century.* New York: Carnegie Corporation.

Chancellor, W. (1904). *Our schools: Their administration and supervision.* Boston: Heath.

Charles, C. M. (2001). *Building classroom discipline.* New York: Longman.

Costa, A., & Guditus, C. (1984). Do districtwide supervisors make a difference? *Educational Leadership, 41,* 23–26.

Cremin, L. (1964). *Transformation of the school: Progressivism in American education, 1876–1957.* New York: Random House.

Cremin, L. (1991). *Popular education and its discontents.* New York: HarperCollins.

Danielson, C. (1996). *Enhancing professional practice: A framework for teaching.* Alexandria, VA: Association for Supervision and Curriculum Development.

Denham, C., & Michael, J. (1981). Teacher sense of efficacy: An important factor in school improvement. *The Elementary School Journal, 86,* 173–184.

Dewey, J. (1899). *The school and society.* Chicago: University of Chicago Press.

Dyer, T. J. (1991). Restructuring the role of the assistant principal. *NASSP, 56*, 58–63.

Educational Testing Service. (1992). *The second international assessment of educational progress.* Princeton, NJ: Educational Testing Service.

Elsbree, W. S., & Reutter, E. E. (1954). *Staff personnel in the public schools.* Englewood Cliffs, NJ: Prentice Hall.

Fenstermacher, G. D. (1994). The knower and the known: The nature of knowledge in research on teaching. In L. Darling-Hammond (Ed.), *Review of research in education.* Washington, DC: American Educational Research Association.

Fitzpatrick, F. A. (1893). How to improve the work of inefficient teachers. *National Educational Association Proceedings, 31*, 71–78.

Foote, C. S., Vermette, P. J., & Battaglia, C. F. (2001). *Constructivist strategies: Meeting standards and engaging adolescent minds.* Larchmont, NY: Eye on Education.

Fullan, M. (1995). In M. J. O'Hair & S. J. Odell (Eds.), *Educating teachers for leadership and change* (pp. 1–10). Thousand Oaks, CA: Corwin Press.

Fullan, M., & Hargreaves, A. (1996). *What's worth fighting for in your school.* New York: Teachers College Press.

Gilland, T. M. (1935). *The origins and development of the powers and duties of the city-school superintendent.* Chicago: University of Chicago Press.

Glanz, J. (1989). The Snoopervisor. *Learning, 89*, 36–37.

Glanz, J. (1991). *Bureaucracy and professionalism: The evolution of public school supervision.* Rutherford, NJ: Fairleigh Dickinson University Press.

Glanz, J. (1994a). Dilemmas of assistant principals in their supervisory role: Reflections of an assistant principal. *Journal of School Leadership, 4*(5), 577–593.

Glanz, J. (1994b). Redefining the roles and responsibilities of assistant principals. *The Clearing House, 67*(5), 283–287.

Glanz, J. (1995). A school/curricular intervention martial arts program for students at risk. *The Journal of At-Risk Issues, 2*(1), 18–25.

Glanz, J. (1998). Histories, antecedents, and legacies—Constructing a history of school supervision. *Handbook of Research on School Supervision* (pp. 39–79). New York: Macmillan Publishers.

Glanz, J. (2003). *Finding your leadership style: A guide for educators.* Alexandria, VA: Association for Supervision and Curriculum Development.

Glatthorn, A. A. (1994). *Developing a quality curriculum.* Alexandria, VA: Association for Supervision and Curriculum Development.

Glatthorn, A. A. (2000). *The principal as curriculum leader* (2nd ed.). Thousand Oaks, CA: Corwin Press.

Glickman, C. D., Gordon, S. P., & Ross-Gordon, J. M. (1998). *Supervision of instruction: A developmental approach.* Boston: Allyn & Bacon.

Glickman, C. D., Gordon, S. P., & Ross-Gordon, J. M. (2004). *Supervision of instruction: A developmental approach* (5th ed.). Boston: Allyn & Bacon.

Goldhammer, R. (1969). *Clinical supervision: Special methods for the supervision of teachers.* New York: Holt, Rinehart, & Winston.

Goldhammer, R., Anderson, R. H., & Krajewski, R. J. (1993). *Clinical supervision: Special methods for the supervision of teachers* (3rd ed.). Fort Worth, TX: Harcourt Brace Jovanovich.

Good, T. L., & Brophy, J. E. (1997). *Looking in classrooms* (7th ed.). Thousand Oaks, CA: Corwin Press.

Gorton, R. A., & Kettman, B. (1985). The assistant principal: An underused asset. *Principal, 65,* 36–40.

Griffin, G. A. (1997). Is staff development supervision? No. In J. Glanz & R. F. Neville (Eds.), *Educational supervision: Perspectives, issues, and controversies* (pp. 162–169). Norwood, MA: Christopher-Gordon.

Hartzell, G. N., Williams, R. C., & Nelson, K. T. (1995). *New voices in the field: The work lives of first-year assistant principals.* Thousand Oaks, CA: Corwin Press.

Hassenpflug, A. (1991). A wasted reform resource: The assistant principal. *Education Week, 23,* 25.

Hill, C. (1992). Foreword. In C. D. Glickman, *Supervision in transition: 1992 Yearbook of the Association for Supervision and Curriculum Development.* Washington, DC: Association for Supervision and Curriculum Development.

Holmes Group. (1986). *Tomorrow's teachers: A report of the Holmes Group.* East Lansing, MI: Holmes Group.

Hunter, M. (1983). *Mastery teaching.* Thousand Oaks, CA: Corwin Press.

Jackson, P. W. (1990). *Life in classrooms.* New York: Teachers College Press.

Johnson, D. W., & Johnson, R. T. (1989). *Cooperation and competition: Theory and practice.* Minneapolis, MN: Interaction.

Kliebard, H. M. (1987). *The struggle for the American curriculum: 1893–1958.* New York: Routledge & Kegan Paul.

Koru, J. M. (1993). The assistant principal: Crisis manager, custodian, or visionary? *NASSP Bulletin, 77,* 67–71.

Kounin, J. (1977). *Discipline and group management in classrooms.* New York: Holt, Rinehart, & Winston.

Krug, E. A. (1964). *The shaping of the American high school, 1890–1920.* New York: Harper & Row.

Lambert, L. (1998). *Building leadership capacity in schools.* Alexandria, VA: Association for Supervision and Curriculum Development.

Liftig, R. (1990). Our dirty little secrets: Myths about teachers and administrators. *Educational Leadership, 47,* 23–26.

Lipham, J. M., Rankin, R. E., & Hoeh, J. A., Jr. (1985). *The principalship.* New York: Longman.

Lucio, W. H., & McNeil, J. D. (1969). *Supervision: A synthesis of thought and action.* New York: McGraw-Hill.

Mamchak, P. S., & Mamchak, S. R. (1983). *School administrator's public speaking portfolio.* Englewood Cliffs, NJ: Center for Applied Research in Education/Prentice Hall.

Marshall, C. (1992). *The assistant principal: Leadership choices and challenges.* Thousand Oaks, CA: Corwin Press.

Marshall, C., & Rossman, G. B. (1999). *Designing qualitative research* (3rd ed.). Newbury Park, CA: Sage.

Marzano, R. J., Pickering, D. J., & Pollock, J. E. (2001). *Classroom instruction that works: Research-based strategies for increasing student achievement.* Alexandria, VA: Association for Supervision and Curriculum Development.

McEwan, E. K. (2003). *Seven steps to effective instructional leadership.* Thousand Oaks, CA: Corwin Press.

NAESP (National Association of Elementary School Principals). (1970). *The assistant principalship in public elementary schools: A research study.* Washington, DC: Author.

National Association of Elementary School Principals. (1970). *The assistant principal.* Alexandria, VA: Author.

National Commission on Excellence in Education. (1983). *A nation at risk: The imperative for educational reform.* Washington, DC: U.S. Department of Education.

Pajak, E. (2000). *Approaches to clinical supervision: Alternatives for improving instruction.* Norwood, MA: Christopher-Gordon.

Payne, W. H. (1875). *Chapters on school supervision.* New York: Wilson, Hinkle & Company.

Pellicer, L. O., & Stevenson, K. R. (1991). The assistant principalship as a legitimate terminal career alternative. *NASSP Bulletin, 71,* 59–65.

Pinar, W. F., Reynolds, W. A., Slattery, P., & Taubman, P. M. (1995). *Understanding curriculum.* New York: Peter Lang.

Ravitch, D. (1995). *National standards in American education: A citizen's guide.* Washington, DC: Brookings Institution.

Reller, T. L. (1935). *The development of the city superintendency of schools in the United States.* Philadelphia: Author.

Robbins, P., & Alvy, H. B. (2003). *The principal's companion: Strategies and hints to make the job easier.* Thousand Oaks, CA: Corwin Press.

Rodgers, C. (2002). Seeing student learning: Teacher change and the role of reflection. *Harvard Educational Review, 72*(2), 230–253.

Sanders, J. R. (2000). *Evaluating school programs: An educator's guide* (2nd ed.). Newbury Park, CA: Corwin Press.

Schubert, W. H. (1993). Curriculum reform. In *Challenges and achievements of American education: The 1993 ASCD yearbook.* Washington, DC: Association for Supervision and Curriculum Development.

Schumaker, D. R., & Sommers, W. A. (2001). *Being a successful principal: Riding the wave of change without drowning.* Thousand Oaks, CA: Corwin Press.

Seguel, M. L. (1966). *The curriculum field: Its formative years.* New York: Teachers College Press.

Sergiovanni, T. J. (1992). Moral authority and the regeneration of supervision. In C. D. Glickman (Ed.), *Supervision in transition* (pp. 30–40). Alexandria, VA: Association for Supervision and Curriculum Development.

Simpson, P. R. (2000). *Assistant principal's survival guide: Practical guidelines and materials for managing all areas of your work.* Paramus, NJ: Prentice Hall.

Sloyer, M. W. (1928). Subject supervision. *Education, 48,* 429.

Spaulding, F. (1955). *School superintendent in action in five cities.* Ringe, NH: Richard R. Smith.

Strober, M., & Tyack, D. B. (1980). Why do women teach and men manage? *Signs, 3,* 30–42.

Sullivan, S., & Glanz, J. (1999). *Supervision that improves teaching: Strategies and techniques.* Thousand Oaks, CA: Corwin Press.

Sullivan, S., & Glanz, J. (2004). *Supervision that improves teaching: Strategies and techniques* (2nd ed.). Thousand Oaks, CA: Corwin Press.

Tanner, D., & Tanner, L. (1987). *Supervision in education: Problems and practices.* New York: Macmillan.

Tyler, R. W. (1949). *Basic principles of curriculum and instruction.* Chicago: University of Chicago Press.

Ubben, G. C., Norris, C. J., & Hughes, L. W. (2000). *The principal: Creative leadership for effective schools.* Boston: Allyn & Bacon.

U.S. Bureau of the Census. (1960). *Historical statistics of the United States: Colonial times to 1957.* Washington, DC: U.S. Government Printing Office.

Vygotski, L. S. (1986). *Thought and language.* Cambridge: MIT Press.

Walber, H. J., Paschal, R. A., & Weinstein, T. (1985). Homework's powerful effects on learning. *Educational Leadership,* 76–79.

Weller, L. D., & Weller, S. J. (2002). *The assistant principal: Essentials for effective leadership.* Thousand Oaks, CA: Corwin Press.

Weller, R. (1971). *Verbal communication in instructional supervision.* New York: Teachers College Press.

Wholey, J. S., Hatry, H. P., & Newcomer, K. E. (1994). *Handbook of practical program evaluation.* San Francisco: Jossey-Bass.

Wiles, J., & Bondi, J. (1991). *Supervision: A guide to practice.* New York: Macmillan.

Willerman, M., McNeely, S. L., & Cooper-Koffman, E. (1991). *Teachers helping teachers: Peer observation and assistance.* New York: Praeger.

Index